WWW.NETWORKTOEMPOWERWOMEN.ORG

MARCHIENE & LEIGH

COPYRIGHT © 2003 BY MARCHIENE & LEIGH.

LIBRARY OF CONGRESS NUMBER: 2003095394
ISBN: HARDCOVER   1-4134-2385-X
      SOFTCOVER   1-4134-2384-1

All rights reserved. No part of this book may be reproduced or transmitted in any form or by any means, electronic or mechanical, including photocopying, recording, or by any information storage and retrieval system, without permission in writing from the copyright owner.

This book was printed in the United States of America.

To order additional copies of this book, contact:
Xlibris Corporation
1-888-795-4274
www.Xlibris.com
Orders@Xlibris.com
19883

CONTENTS

GRATITUDES AND DEDICATION 7

INTRODUCTION: *LET'S FLY WITH BOTH WINGS* 9

CHAPTER ONE: *THE POWER OF OUR STORIES* 21

CHAPTER TWO: *REAL POWER AND HOW TO USE IT* 37

CHAPTER THREE: *THE POWER OF SACRED CIRCLES* 58

CHAPTER FOUR: *THE POWER OF QUESTIONING* 72

CHAPTER FIVE: *THE POWER OF EXPERIENCE* 102

CHAPTER SIX: *THE POWER OF TRUE PARTNERSHIP* .. 132

CHAPTER SEVEN: *FUTURE POWER* 154

CHAPTER EIGHT: *THE POWER OF OUR MYTHS* 168

CHAPTER NINE: *THE POWER OF YOUR CHOOSING* 186

BIBLIOGRAPHY 199

RESOURCE APPENDIX 201

CIRCLE MEETING GUIDES 210

THIS BOOK IS DEDICATED TO ALL THE WOMEN AND MEN
WHOSE HEARTS CATCH FIRE WHEN THEY READ IT,
AND IN WHOSE LIVES THE VISION OF EQUAL PARTNERSHIP
TAKES ROOT AND GROWS.

The simple nine questions found in this book can transform the way you think about yourself and empower you in your relationships. Just as 12-step groups have helped millions of people gain control of their lives, N.E.W. groups have the potential to help countless women and men who desire to live more authentic lives.

Sharon Miller, Ph.D.
Center for the Study of Theological Education,
Auburn Theological Seminary, New York

GRATITUDES and DEDICATION

To begin with, I am grateful to all the women who encouraged me to initiate the Network to Empower Women and write this book. Without their support, I could not have done it.

I am especially grateful to Bonnie, who hosted the first N.E.W. circle meeting at her home and urged me to start women's circles in our community right away to test the material I was writing; to Ai Gvhdi Waya, who lit a fire under me to write this book as soon as possible, and models for me what it means to be a powerful woman empowering other women; to Donna, who has been my encouraging and creative partner in this whole process, providing her wonderful art, her encouraging words, and her unstinting inspiration for the book and the N.E.W. circles; to Ruth and Marianna, who generously provided the perfect spaces in which our pioneering women's circles could meet; to all the women who consistently attended the first two N.E.W. circles and provided invaluable feedback; and to my readers: Lillian, Donna, John, Debra, Ghazala, Ai Gvhdi Waya, Sharon, and Karen. Their thoughtful suggestions and affirmations have made this a better book in many ways. When I think of all those, both named and unnamed, who have so generously given of themselves and their precious time, my heart overflows with thanksgiving.

Finally, I want to thank my husband John, whose supportive partnership and unfailing generosity have always enabled me to follow my dreams.

INTRODUCTION

LET'S FLY WITH BOTH WINGS

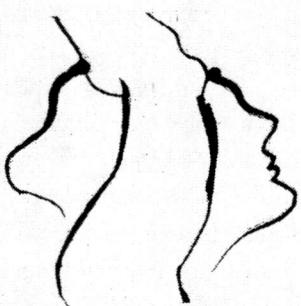

I was walking through the woods one day, not long ago. The path was made for walking meditation, and on the trees were signs painted with memorable words from people of great spirit. I was stopped in my tracks by one in particular:

> *"The human race is like a bird trying to fly with one wing. Until women fly alongside men using all their gifts, this bird cannot fly."*

These words gave me a great deal to ponder as I continued through the woods. Pictures of the news flashed in my head: world leaders meeting, with only a few women among them; political and business leaders meeting, and among them, only a token woman or two. I could not remember seeing a picture of any important meeting of the top leaders in any field that was not completely, or almost completely, made up of men. It seemed that women were conspicuous by their absence in any significant numbers in those places where the decisions that shape the world are made.

" Something is wrong with this picture," I thought to myself. " At least half of the faces in those pictures should be women! After all, they are half the population. They hold up half the sky, as the Chinese proverb puts it. They have so much wisdom, so many gifts that aren't being used to help create a better future for this world. Almost everywhere, they are burdened with most of the home responsibilities, and labor under limits that don't allow them to fly alongside men. This must change! I need to do something about it! But what?"

Over the next few months, in stages, I was given clear guidance in answer to my question. Someone recommended the book *The Soul's Code* by James Hillman. The basic idea is that each of us is born with a certain built-in purpose, and the gifts to fulfill that purpose. He uses the image of the acorn, which contains in it the whole pattern for the oak it can become. The book contains many stories of well-known people who discovered and lived out their "soul's code." It might be a particular kind of work, or it might be the unique pattern and style a person lived.

I lived for weeks wondering, "What is my soul's code?" All the while, I was keenly aware of how fortunate I was to even be able to ask the question with some hope of not only discovering the answer, but also living it out when I did. So many people do not live in circumstances that are friendly to this quest. They are barely surviving, or they live in social groups that squelch non-conformity.

But I knew I needed to keep seeking the answer to my question. It came one day when I was sitting in an armchair, holding my grandson Gabriel—a baby born to my oldest son John and his wife Michelle after they tried for years to have children. They had almost given up when he was conceived. Now, here he was, a healthy beautiful baby, sleeping in my arms. An inspiration came to me as I gazed at his angelic face. "Gabriel," I whispered. "You have an angel's name—an angel who came with special messages from God for human beings. Tell me, what is my soul's code?"

Immediately the answer came, like a clear bell ringing in the crystal air of a silent dawn. "It is to empower women." It was a moment of truth. My heart resonated in response to it. I knew it was so. I had sensed it for a long time, but not with this kind of clarity and strength. "Thank-you," I whispered as I kissed Gabriel. I sat holding him and the answer I had been given as winter sunlight streamed through a great tree framed by the window across from me, creating a wonderful pattern of shadows on the golden wood floor. Then the question opened up to reveal another inside it. "How am I meant to empower women now?"

My mind flew back to my childhood in India and Pakistan, where as a girl I had seen how girls and women were less valued than men, more confined, limited, and unfairly treated over and over again. When my brother was born, for example, all kinds of people came over to congratulate my parents, and bring gifts. When my little sister was born, only a few showed up, offering condolences! This was only one of many ways in which I experienced how girls and women were put at a big disadvantage from birth onwards. My innate sense of fairness was outraged. In my little girl's heart, I vowed fiercely that I would fight against this any way I could.

Never did I allow any comment from my playmates, classmates, or anyone, to go unchallenged if it implied that girls were inferior in any way because of our gender. I took pride in being one of the best students and fastest runners in my class. Once, I challenged a bishop's son to a fight on the playground when he had pulled my pigtails and pestered me once too often. I won, and wasn't bothered again by him or any boy. This experience taught me that girls could defend themselves and refuse to be treated badly.

I often found myself defending girlfriends as well as myself. As I grew older, I would reproach them when they spoke or acted as if they were inferior, or not capable of something because of their gender. My favorite song back then was a spiritual with the words, "If anybody asks you who you are, tell them you're the image of God!" Somehow, the profound truth of that song penetrated my young soul and I wanted it to penetrate the souls of everyone I knew. I was convinced it would make things fair and right for girls and women. I still believe that. It's just that the full meaning of this truth hasn't penetrated enough souls yet! When it does, girls and women will be treated everywhere with respect and honor, and encouraged to use all their gifts.

My parents returned from India to live in the United States when I was fourteen years old. I discovered that while it was a bit subtler, the same basic disadvantages of being female were in place in the country my parents called home. For instance, ever since I was a little girl, I wanted to be a minister. In the fifties in Grand Rapids, Michigan, that was unthinkable for a woman to aspire to. As a vulnerable teenager, I did not want to be too different, for fear of total rejection. So I said very little about my childhood dream, and settled for teaching, since that was approved of by the people around me.

Years later, when I was married and a young mother, I had several experiences which convinced me that I was still being Divinely led to be a minister, and must do it, in spite of the opposition. I enrolled at the nearest seminary, and began focusing on preparing for the work I wanted to do: preaching and leading worship, spiritual counseling, teaching, and the like. I was the first woman at Calvin Seminary to graduate with the Master of Divinity degree, but the Christian Reformed Church, of which I was a member, refused to consider me as a candidate for ministry. Fortunately, the Presbyterians accepted me into their fold, and I became the founding pastor of a new church.

I began to realize that as a woman minister challenging the church to allow women to use their gifts as God led them, I was a source of inspiration and empowerment to many women watching from the sidelines. "If she can do it—maybe I can too," they thought. Some did go on to become ministers, and others pursued different dreams, having become convinced that it was right and good to do so. I was often told, as the years went on, that it was simply my "doing it" and challenging the religious and social rules that kept women in "their place" which gave other women the impetus to do the same. It also changed many men's minds about what women could or should do.

Over and over again, in heart-to-heart talks with women who came to me, and in public speeches addressed to the powers-that-be, I urged women and men to realize what wonderful things could happen in the world, religious institutions, and the home, if women and men became genuine partners. In my home, my husband supported my "call" and was willing to share in more of the care-taking tasks of home and family. It took some negotiation, and it was not ideal, but it was a much better situation. We had two sons and two daughters, and brought them up to live by the ideals I was voicing in public.

Recently, my second son, Ron, who is the father of three little children, and who shares equally in their care and the care of the home, told me, "Mom, women can't be empowered to use all their gifts in the world if men don't use their gifts in the home, and equally share the housework and child care. In other words, women can't do it alone." I could not have agreed more. It was real partnership I was longing for, for the sake of women, men, children, and the whole world.

All of this flashed through my mind as I sat in my oldest son's living room, holding a grandbaby in my arms, pondering what to do next to empower women. I was in a different stage in my life. I was not tied to any religious institution anymore, and I was free of the responsibilities of my earlier years in the home and workplace. I waited for guidance from that same inner Wisdom which answered my question about my soul's code.

It came during a four-day time of solitude and reflection at Morningstar, my favorite retreat center. As I left the house for Morningstar, I pulled a book off my shelf entitled *Now It's our Turn: How Women Can Transform Their Lives and Save the Planet* by Alana Lyons. Once settled into Gabriel's cabin, (yes, that was it's name!) I curled up by the fire, and read from my journals and the book. Together, they lit a flame of inspiration in my heart and sent sparks of ideas flying through my mind. I took a long walk through the woods, pondering all I had read. Then I sat in silence for a long time, not thinking, just being.

Finally, up from the depths came these thoughts: "Wouldn't it be wonderful if everywhere in the world there were women's circles meeting, which provided a process for empowering women. Any woman who wanted support could go to a meeting in her area. It would be like all the twelve-step groups that meet in so many places to help people with various kinds of addictions. **Only—the purpose and process would be different**. The purpose would be to empower women to be all they can be for their own sakes, and the sake of the flourishing of the world. The process would be nine questions instead of twelve steps because questions leave things open-ended and encourage the questioner to explore her own experience, beliefs, and inner wisdom."

These insights led to talks with women friends who had been in self-help groups, and others who were writers, therapists, social workers, artists, ministers, and homemakers, among other things. With their excited encouragement, I kept exploring what could be. Gradually, the vision of what I was to do took shape. The name for it was: **N.E.W.: Network to Empower Women.**

I realized how important it is for women to connect with each other for the purpose of empowering one another, with no apologies for doing so! I observed that too many women are divided among themselves, often isolated (particularly in Western culture) and lacking in solidarity and support for one another. Many still compete with each other for male attention. Their lack of solidarity with each other is a major roadblock in making progress. Yet, I saw that when women do get together to support each other's progress in living with true power, and making changes in their lives and their world, important things happened. It made a huge difference.

Hence, a **network** was needed, made up of circles of women meeting everywhere, and a web site which would connect them with each other, as well as a myriad of resources and other organizations already helping to empower women. (The Resource Appendix and the web site list some of these organizations and resources.)

In my conversations with women and men about my NEW project, the subject of empowerment proved to be tricky. Some men and women felt that if women were empowered, men would be dis-empowered. As we talked, I came to see that it was crucial to understand true power in contrast to false power.

In most societies today, power is considered to be, when it comes right down to it, the ability to make things happen as one wants them to, whether by force or otherwise. It is often experienced by the less "powerful" as domination, and the Status Quo is exactly that: the domination of the many by the few through the use of economic, political, social, religious, and other forces. I say "forces" deliberately, because that is what false power always boils down to: force, or the threat of it, however subtle it may be. This kind of power is weak at the core. It is destructive, not constructive, and based on fear rather than love.

True power is the ability to choose, create, and act for one's own flourishing, and the flourishing of all others, including creation. It is rooted in love and is creative. The most awesome power is the power to create life; and then to sustain it and help it flourish. Women already have this ability, this wonderful power. It is their birthright. They just have not used this power for many centuries as fully as they could, because of the false beliefs that have such a grip on so many human minds and hearts.

To **empower** women, then, is simply to remind them of the true power that is already theirs, and encourage them to use it fully. This in no way harms men or anyone or anything else! In fact, it will help create a world far better than the one we now live in. The state of the world today is witness to the sad truth that false power is exercised far more often than true power. False power is destructive of life because it depends on force. Unfortunately, it is quicker and easier to destroy and spoil life than to create and sustain life. For example, think how quickly a person can be killed. Then think of all the effort it takes to birth and raise a child to adulthood. Since true power creates and sustains life, it takes greater effort, more time, and co-operation. But it is well worth it. When men and women together, as partners in all arenas of society, exercise true power with and for each other and the world, wonderful things can happen. That is the overall vision of this book and the movement I hope it launches. I believe there is hope. Human beings chose this state of affairs, and they can choose to change it. Crucial to that change, I believe, is the empowerment of women, so that they can use all their wisdom and gifts in every arena of society, not just some. When more women realize that true power is innate, a part of their nature, and that they can use it, they will. When more men realize that true power is a far better choice than false power, and are willing to act with true power for the flourishing of all, the world will be a much better place, because balance will finally be restored. The bird that is humanity will finally be able to fly, because it is flying with both wings, male and female.

I believe this can happen, and I know that my "soul's code" is to do what I can to help it happen. Therefore, I am writing this book to help launch the Network to Empower Women. Just as the Blue Book is used to guide twelve step groups, I envision this N.E.W. Book as a guide and inspiration to N.E.W. circles and everyone who in some way shares the vision I have described.

In this book, I will tell why I believe there is hope, based on important knowledge about our past as women, and what is happening to empower women the world over at the present time. I will explore more deeply what the nature of true power is, and how it can be used in our individual lives, in our homes, in our relationships, in the work place, and in the larger world. I will explore the power of meeting in circles, explaining what they are, how they best function, and why, and what can happen through "circle power." My experience in starting and working with N.E.W. circles will be described, and a clear model provided so that anyone can start and sustain a N.E.W. circle.

As I have talked about my N.E.W. project with family, friends, and women who have joined N.E.W. circles, the question arises over and over again, "But what about men?" The focus is on circles for women in the first place, because they cannot come to the table, so to speak, as full partners, until they fully realize and exercise their own power. Then they can meet with men in circles if they so choose. Meanwhile, men can also meet in circles using the process described in this book. Chapter six goes into more detail on why and how this can happen, since this book is about empowering women for partnership with men, after all. Men's empowerment in the sense of true power is important too. Bashing men or ignoring them is no better than the treatment women have gotten over the centuries! Our present disastrous state of affairs is not the fault of men so much as it is the fault of a horrible set of beliefs, many of them unconscious, which need to be examined and thrown into the scrap-heap of history. I'll examine those too—and ways to rid ourselves of them.

The heart of this book is the Nine Questions. Everything in the book relates to one or more of these questions. They are like tools that open up what the rest of the book says. Even more important, they are a means to explore *your own* experience and wisdom. Harry Palmer, in his book

THE FUTURE FOR WOMEN - A N.E.W. BOOK

Love Precious Humanity, says, " Wisdom is like stiff clay; you have to work it with your own hands before it becomes useful." Think of the Nine Questions as a way for you to do that.

Finally, I will provide a modest selection of resources: books, magazines, videos and movies, drama, music, art, organizations, retreat centers, and web sites that empower women. This will include the N.E.W. Website, which will be up and running when this book is published.

The book will end with a couple of stories that express, in a symbolic way, what N.E.W. is all about.

Your response as readers of this book is very important to me, and you are encouraged to go to the N.E.W. website: *www. Networktoempowerwomen.org.* or email me at: *marchiene@earthlink.net* or write me at: Marchiene Rienstra, Box 398, Douglas, MI 49406(USA) with your insights, illustrations, questions, and comments.

I am keenly aware that this book reflects my perspective as a white American woman. Even though I have lived for years in other countries, it is inevitable that my experience and culture shape this book. I have tried to be as inclusive as possible. But I know my limitations! Those of you whose experience is different because you come from other cultures and religious, social, or economic contexts may want to test the material in this book, and discover how it might be modified to better fit the needs of women with whom you are familiar. I would highly value your input, so that a future version of this book could be more multi-cultural in its approach, and therefore better suited to a wider variety of women worldwide. In short, I need the help of you who are my sisters living in contexts very different from what is most familiar to me. Together, we can create the best possible material for empowering women.

My hope is that N.E.W. will become a growing movement, requiring that this book go through several revisions, which will include your contributions. I look forward to a wonderful N.E.W. partnership that will help all our lives and the life of the world truly flourish.

The cover art and the art inside this book are vital to its message. Here are the artist's words about the images she provided for this book. Notice that at the end of each chapter, you will find one of her wonderful images of women, followed by a blank page for you to use to write or draw what is in your heart and mind after reading the chapter. In this way, I hope that you will make this book truly your own.

Donna Leigh:

> "The cover art symbolically represents the balance and connection that we, as women, can strive to obtain in our relationships with the feminine and masculine within and without ourselves, in order to manifest a more peaceful and balanced world. The dancer's posture is one of the movements in this dance of wholeness. The nine circles individually, and the circular structure of the picture as a whole, reflect the N.E.W. process of meeting in circles, using Nine Questions, and repeating the process in a way that deepens reflection and transformation. One Question is at the center of each circle meeting. There are nine of them, because nine symbolizes the time it takes a woman to gestate and then birth new life; and nine (three times three) is also symbolic of the ancient feminine trinity of maiden, mother, and wise elder or crone.
>
> The colors of white, red, and black also symbolize this trinity. White represents woman as maiden; red represents woman as mother; and black represents woman as grandmother/crone. The word form Wo/men is used in the title to express the partnership of both genders necessary in order to achieve a flourishing future for the earth. N.E.W. stands for the Network to Empower Women—a movement this book is intended to launch."

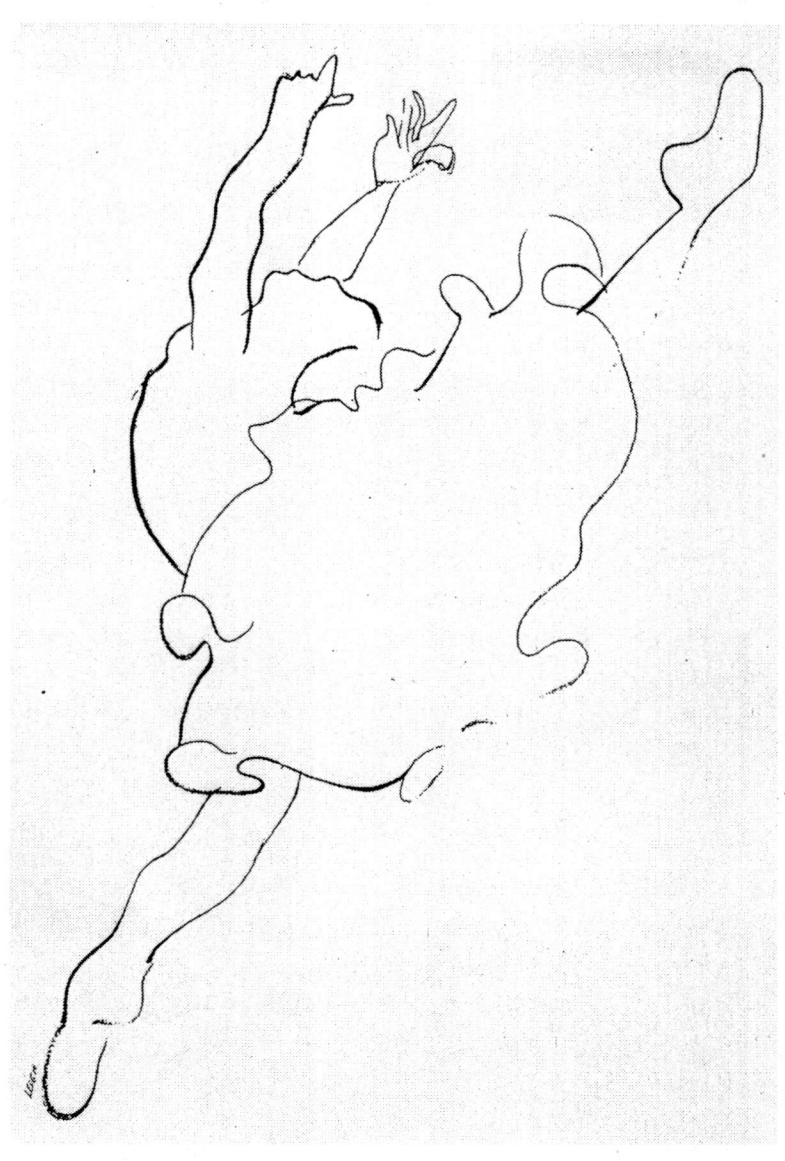

CHAPTER ONE

THE POWER OF OUR STORIES

    I have told you a piece of my story in the introduction, because I think it is so important that we women tell each other our stories. And when those stories are told from the heart, with integrity and honesty, they are sacred. A friend of mine, Tom, used this memorable phrase: "Our sacred stories are bushes burning in the wilderness of time." We can hear the Divine Voice in them when we listen with our hearts, just as Moses heard it in the burning bush in the wilderness. (The Hebrew Bible, Exodus 3)

Tragically, we do not always value our stories. That is because so much of our story as women has been erased from history. What we learned in school is indeed "his-story." Most of the stories have been about men, made up by men, and from men's viewpoints. The viewpoint of women is largely missing. What happened to "her-story?"

When the belief began to prevail that women's lives were less important, and therefore less worth remembering and recording than men's lives, their stories were ignored or even erased. They were erased based on the false and damaging belief that the world should be led and shaped by men, because women and girls were weaker, inferior, and existed mainly for the support and benefit of men. Evidence to the contrary from the lives of women was not usually welcome in the "official" records. If you do a little research, you will find all kinds of quotes by men that provide ample evidence for these beliefs. Here is just one example: "If woman were not bodily and mentally weak, she would be extremely dangerous." (Dr. Moebius from Treatise *on the Imbecility of Women,* 1901.) Many more could be cited, but if it is true that what you give your attention to expands, I don't want to give any more attention to quotes like these. They deserve to be forgotten!

However, if you look out at the world today, you will see many evidences that such beliefs still have far more influence than they should. There is not one of us who has not seen such evidence if we look with clear eyes at our society and beyond. It was not always so. New and extensive research by archeologists has revealed a pre-historic past in which things were very different from the way they have been for most of recorded history.

Five thousand and more years ago, there were many societies in which women and men lived as partners. The Divinity was imaged mainly as a great Mother, who gave life to all that existed. Life was valued above all, and there is little evidence of warfare in the archeological remains that have been uncovered. People seemed to have lived peacefully in places like present-day Eastern Europe, Turkey, Crete, Malta, and in parts of Russia, China, and India. Children were traced through the mother's lineage, rather than the father's, and husbands lived with their wives' family and clan. There was no great difference between rich and poor; no evidence of houses and graves much grander and greater than others.

Land was communally held and farmed. Women and men together invented agriculture, the arts, medicine, pottery, domestication of animals, and much more. Women and men together led religious rituals, with women often taking the lead, as those who bore life, and thus most closely resembled the great Mother Godde. (* I use this spelling for the Divinity to include the feminine nature of God neglected in traditional religious language.)

The art of the time shows a great reverence for nature—the soil, rocks, plants, trees, and birds, fish, and animals of all kind. There are no scenes of warfare, of kings with people in chains being taken into captivity, or any hint of the glorification of warfare and the warrior king that is found in later art.

All over the world, there are legends in various cultures of a Golden Age when people lived like this: at peace, with plenty for all, and a full equality between women and men, along with a deep respect for life in all its forms. (For a full recounting of the historical and archeological evidence for this period, see *The Language of the Goddess* by Marija Gimbutas)

There are also ancient stories of how the change for the worse came about. The account of the Fall in Genesis in the Bible is the most familiar in our society. There are many interpretations of this story, but it is clear that the relationship between male and female went from harmony, balance, and love to one in which the male accused and dominated the female. With this change came violence, murder, rape, disease, and all the rest of the sad story. The ancient myths of many cultures depict these changes in graphic terms.

Basic to all of them was a change in belief. In the "Golden Age" the belief was that the best way for men and women and nature to live together was in harmony and balance and co-operation, with the welfare of all in mind at all times. Then the belief changed to the idea that the best way for men, women, and nature to live together was for a few men to dominate other men, all women and children, and nature. In books like *The Chalice and the Blade*, by Riane Eisler, this change is described in detail with much compelling evidence. In spite of the evidence, those who wish to keep the Status Quo intact have not welcomed this different perspective on human history. After all, if it is true that there were once societies in which there was full partnership between men and women, and a peaceful, flourishing one at that, with none of the poverty and violence we take for granted now—then it could happen again. And if it did, there would have to be huge changes in the Status Quo.

The powers-that-be would prefer that we believe what we have been told for a long time: that human beings have always been cruel and violent; that warfare is inevitable; that men have always dominated women; that there have always been rich and poor; that society has always been a hierarchy with a few rich and powerful men at the top. This is how it is and always was and always will be, they say. And if we believe it, as too many people have for too long, of course, there is no hope for a real change. For what we believe, deep down, determines what we think, feel, and do.

But, if the new archeological evidence is true, and I believe it is, then we have reason to hope that our world could once again be the peaceful, flourishing place it was for everyone who lived in it. I have personally been enormously empowered by the evidence of women's power and equality long ago, and the beautiful, strong images of women from the art of that prehistoric time. It is vitally important in our world today for us as women (and men too) to know our "herstory" and integrate it into our own stories and lives, so that we can live in a way that is congruent with who we really are—life-giving, powerful, wise, wonderful women without whose full participation this world will perish.

I have also been encouraged by discovering that here in the United States, there are tribes of Native Americans whose traditions were quite similar to the prehistoric people described above. The Cherokee, for instance, always had more women than men in the governing council that decided whether or not to go to war against other tribes. They realized the women would be sending their own husbands and sons into battle, and they also knew from experience that the balance of women's perspective as those who bore life at no small sacrifice was needed to counter the greater aggressive tendencies of the men. Among the Iroquois, a woman's council could depose a male chief who was not leading the people in a way they judged best for all. There were women chiefs among some of the tribes, and among almost all of them, a belief in the crucial importance of balance between male and female energies for the good of the earth and all its inhabitants. (For more on the ways in which the ancient peoples of the Americas balanced male and female power, see *Buffalo Woman Comes Singing* by Brooke Medicine Eagle, *Voices of Our Ancestors* by Dhyani Ywahoo, and *Indian Givers* by Jack Weatherford.)

It is no accident that these Original Peoples, and Original Peoples all over the world, have suffered greatly at the hands of the dominant cultures where they live. For the dominant cultures are under the sway of beliefs that can be called "the Domination System." This is a system in which power is wielded from the top down, with a few people, usually men, wielding power over all others, in a hierarchically organized society, best symbolized by a pyramid. Under this system, all over the world the ancient, more egalitarian and earth-respecting tribes have been horribly treated, and are still unjustly dominated to this day.

And now what do we see as we look around? In many ways, the Domination System is still very much in control. At the heart of that system is the relationship between men and women. A brief look at the history of the United States is most revealing of the sway of false and damaging beliefs about men and women. The founding mothers of the United States were considered the property of their husbands, and daughters the property of their fathers until they were married. This idea is still reflected in the traditional marriage ceremony in which the father "gives" the bride to the husband, while the mother, who bore her, stands silently by!

Only men were educated in institutions of higher learning, and only men could vote until 1920. It took women seventy years of struggle to win the vote from all-male Congresses! This is in my mother's lifetime—not very long ago. Until 1937 there was a federal ban against birth control. If it were not for the courage and action of American women of previous generations, we might still live without these freedoms we now enjoy.

Abigail Smith Adams, wife of present John Adams, wrote these words to her husband in 1776 as the Second Continental Congress was debating the Declaration of independence: "I long to hear that you have declared an independency, and by the way, in the new code of laws which I suppose it will be necessary for you to make, I desire you would remember the ladies and be more generous and favorable to them than your ancestors. Do not put such unlimited power into the hands of husbands . . . If particular care and attention are not paid to the ladies, we are determined to foment a rebellion, and will not hold ourselves bound to obey any laws in which we have no voice or representation." These are brave words for a woman of that time—and even women of our time. How many of us consider ourselves free of moral obligation to obey the laws of our land, because they were made without our representation? To this day, women are only a small minority in Congress, in state legislatures, and in the executive branch of the government at all levels. Yet we are half or more of the population. And this is supposed to be a democracy! So far, in spite of some progress recently, it is democracy with a male face!

How have women fared under this system? Women hold fewer than five percent of senior management positions in the business world. Today, women generally have more years of schooling than men; yet still make only about 75 cents to every dollar a man makes. Such wage inequality keeps women economically and psychologically dependent upon men for a decent lifestyle, because in general, men are the ones who make the most money and have the better job. While the top (male) heads of corporations make millions of dollars a year, the majority of the poor in America are women and children. In households headed by single and divorced mothers (a growing number) 35% are at or below the poverty line. Many divorced women never receive court-ordered support from ex-husbands. Studies show that only half the amount awarded for child support is ever paid, and the average child support paid is only around $60.00 a month. Who can feed a child a healthy diet, pay for clothes, health care, and education, on that amount?

Things are no better for older women. There are around 50 million older women, and more than half of them live alone. In our culture, such women are treated as disposable. Most have finished rearing children and nourishing husbands and families, and are therefore "useless." Women are valued in our society more for their youth and beauty than for their wisdom. And most can ill afford to retire, because if they do work outside the home, less than 20% of their employers provide private pension arrangements. Moreover, the years a mother might have taken off work to have a child and care for her family are called "zero years" by the Social Security Administration, meaning they carry no monetary benefits. This shows how little our society values women's work within the home and family. (* The information cited above is taken from Alana Lyon's book *Now It's Our Turn.)*

Under this unfair and unbalanced system, the odds do not favor women or children! I think it is a wonder that when women realize what they are up against, they still get married and have children. It is a great risk in our society. And even those women who work outside the home and earn an income must usually do most of the housework and childcare in addition, while earning less than equal pay, and often having to work in conditions where subtle or outright sexism prevails. Too often, they surrender their income to their husband's control so that they do not even enjoy the kind of independence and power a job might give them in their relationship with men.

This inequality can only exist when belief in the "divine right" of men to rule home and society is ruling in the hearts and minds of too many people. Unfortunately, as the term "divine right" implies, religion (all religions to some extent) have historically promoted this idea in one form or another. Women are made to feel that they are fighting God Himself (always Him rather than Her) if they struggle to change things. That is the experience of our foremothers in this country, that is my experience, and the experience of many women in this country and all over the world.

It is important to realize that religion, because it is always imbedded in culture and society, not only shapes but is also shaped by them. There is a great deal in world religions and spiritualities that nourishes the human soul, and offers Divine wisdom and guidance for life that is of great value. Women have often been the majority of faithful followers in many world religions, and have both contributed to and been inspired and helped by them. I personally have been moved, deepened, and inspired by the truths I have discovered in world religions.

On the other hand, the fact is that the world's religions in their institutional form have also been one of the chief sources of women's oppression. Religious beliefs and customs that contradict some of the deepest values of world religions, such as the Golden Rule in all its variations, are to this day instrumental in preserving the unbalanced and unequal relationship between men and women. Very few women are allowed into the top leadership positions in religious institutions, and, with a few exceptions, their wisdom has not historically been included in the religious texts and traditions of world religions.

As long as women, along with men, continue to believe that the present relationship between male and female is what it should be, whether for religious reasons, or other reasons, the Status Quo will continue, and our world will continue on its perilous course towards destruction by warfare or/and environmental catastrophe. A brief look at the fate of women on the planet at this time, and therefore of the planet itself, is sobering.

There are more than 2.5 billion women in the world. In many countries, they are still considered the property of the their father, husband, or even brother. There is inhumane discrimination against women, and they have inferior status in family, and social, political, and economic spheres everywhere. A recent United Nations Development Report states that there is no country where women are treated as well as men.

It is true that upper class women have often had fewer hardships and obstacles of a certain kind than lower class men. However, this book is not about human suffering in general, but the particular suffering of the vast majority of women in all times and places. The incidents of dowry deaths of women in India, of the killing of female infants in Asia, the use of the genital mutilation of girls in Africa, the enforced segregation and limitation of women in many Islamic countries, sexual slavery and prostitution in many societies, and the widespread incidents all over the world of wife beating, rape, and child abuse, (all of which are experienced by women and girls in all strata of society) together give evidence that the lot of females under the present Domination System is a terrible one. I am sure that many of you could tell stories about your own life, and the lives of women you know that would further illustrate this truth.

It is altogether appropriate to be indignant about this state of affairs. I am aware that when I consider the ages-long injustice women have suffered, the horrible suffering they have unjustly endured, and the terrible loss to the world of the things women could have done if they were encouraged to, I feel angry. I am aware that my anger can make people uncomfortable. Women in American culture, and many others, are not supposed to show their anger. They are supposed to be nice, and not make others uncomfortable, especially men. However, psychologists tell us that one of the chief causes of the widespread depression women experience is repressed rage. There is enormous energy in anger, and it can be turned against oneself, or it can be used to attack others, or it can be channeled into taking positive action to change a situation for the better. It is important for us as women to feel our anger at the injustices done to us as a whole, as well as personally, and then to express and channel it in a constructive way. This is much better than always trying to be calm, objective, and thereby deny the reality of how we feel. The energy in our anger is so huge, it can change the world when it is positively directed. That is one of the aims of this book—to provide a positive way to channel our anger, not ignore it.

Fortunately, there is also another side to the picture I have just painted, and it offers hope that our efforts can be fruitful. Even in the past, when far less progress had been made on women's rights, and in places where it was dangerous to even think in such terms, women somehow managed to "buck the system," and make outstanding contributions to the society in which they lived. There have been great women saints, writers, artists, scientists, military leaders, rulers, spiritual leaders, healers—the list could go on and on, and they somehow made it into the history books. In fact, every year in the United States, women's history month is celebrated, because it is important for women, men, and children to realize the wide range of women's wonderful accomplishments in the past, so that the present and future can be shaped accordingly. Libraries are full of books on the subject of what women have done in spite of everything, and recently these facts are even beginning to make it into school curricula at all levels!

When we look about us now, we see a whole new story happening. It is the story of women all over the world, as well as in this country, finding ways to use their innate, life-giving power. Most of them don't make it into the media reports of the "news," but there are magazines and some radio and T.V. channels (like Oxygen) that are featuring these stories. It is important for us to know them, and to be a part of creating them, because they create a momentum for change that is unstoppable.

In our own society, as we look about us, we see all kinds of positive change for women. They have access to all levels of education, and in the relatively short time they have had it, they have progressed to the point that women as a whole are more educated than men as a whole. Although there is still some discrimination against them in education, they have prevailed against it in many ways, and now make up almost half of the population in law schools, medical schools, seminaries, and other places from which women were excluded only a century or less ago! In our lifetimes, women have broken barriers against them in the military, in top business positions, in government, in sports, in the media, and in religion. In any major city, there is a good chance of there being women ministers or rabbis. Major religious bodies, like the Catholic and Orthodox and Baptist churches, Orthodox synagogues, and Muslim mosques still keep women out of the clergy and top positions of leadership, but in the more open and progressive religious organizations, that is no longer the case.

In short, everywhere, you can find stories of girls and women who are coming into their own, challenging the system, and winning. Many young women in this country, especially in the middle and upper classes, have been raised with empowerment talk all along. The idea and experience of fair and equal treatment is not new to them. Even better, they are often supported by men who see the fairness of equal opportunity and equality for women, and are willing to back it. What stories do you know that illustrate all of this? Treasure them, tell them, let them give you hope for the changes that still need to be made for the vast majority of the world's women.

In the world at large, women are also doing important things that are changing the Status Quo. Think of what is happening in Afghanistan, after the fall of the Taliban! And that is only one place. In the Netherlands, women have pushed for equal pay as well as a five-hour workday, so that their work outside the home as well as inside the home can be equally divided. In 1981, 20,000 women went on strike, including the refusal of housewives to make dinner, in order to get their demands met.

In Guyana, women have banded together as the Women's Rights campaign, and presented a draft Domestic Violence Bill to the government. In countries where sex tourism catering to males is big business, women are banding together to stop it. For example, women of the Philippines have started "Gabriela" and women in Thailand have organized the Women's Information Center. International efforts to stop the sex trade have been organized as well.

In Scandinavia, women are putting pressure on the United Nations to help redefine men's roles. They want a U.N. conference entitled "Changing the Role of Men from Dominance to Partnership." The U.N. has already adopted a document entitled the "Convention on the Elimination of All Forms of Discrimination Against Women". It encourages equality between men and women, and realizes that the traditional roles need to change, with women taking more responsibility in society and men taking more responsibility in the family. It encourages giving women a helping hand in governments until there is gender balance. One government to respond positively was Brazil, which in 1996 passed a law requiring that at least 20 percent of all candidates for municipal office be women. So far, this is working. Many nations have already signed this treaty, and many more will—especially as women pressure their governments to do so.

The United Nations also holds periodic conferences on women that set a positive vision for governmental attitudes and policies on women all over the world. The 1995 Conference on Women in Beijing, China produced an official document entitled "The Platform for Action" which is a guide for the actions governments can take to address women's status and well being in their countries and the world.

By and large, the media do not highlight these efforts, because they are run by the leaders of the Status Quo, who are not eager for women or men to see hope for change, to find ways to change, and to connect with each other to create change which challenges the dominant culture. Thank goodness for the Internet, which is full of literally millions of sites created by organizations working in all sorts of ways to empower women. (Many of these can be found in the Resource Appendix at the back of this book.)

I have been recounting facts. Behind every fact are many stories. These are stories full of hope, stories that reflect the change that is needed in the world so that the human species can be a bird flying with both wings. My own story is one of them. When I went to seminary, I was a rare case as a woman. That is no longer true. When I was ordained as a minister in the Presbyterian Church in 1979, there were very few other women ministers to mentor me. That too, has changed. I was asked to be the senior minister of a large church in 1984. That was a rarity then. It is far more common now.

In my experience, many women and men have been most supportive of the equality of women in the church as well as elsewhere. I never paid much attention to those who were not supportive. Why give their view the attention it doesn't deserve? I believe that those who still resist the equality of women, making up whatever backlash there is, are the last gasp of a dying order. The Domination System of power is going to go the way of the dinosaurs, and deservedly so, because it is not advantageous for the survival and welfare of humans, let alone the rest of creation. We are the bridge generation, we who are living today.

My son and his wife and family are an example. My son has always supported the idea of the equality of women and men in home and society. He and his wife have taken turns being the primary caretaker of home and children, depending on who got the best job. Now, they are in a situation in which they both share equally in working professionally and caring for their children and home. The children are far better off for having a good father around much more than the system of the past allowed. Both my son and his wife are happy with their arrangement. Calvin College, for which they work, is to be commended for supporting this arrangement, as are all institutions that do so. I believe more and more will, as the advantages of real partnership of the kind my son and his wife are living become apparent. Everyone wins—men, women, children, and even institutions that are willing to change creatively. They have the great advantage of the gifts of males and females contributing to their well-being. I believe this is the wave of the future. Some couples might not choose this way, or find it possible at a certain stage in their life. But they can be supportive of the idea. As more and more couples are able to share equally in parenting and working in the world, homes will become more stable and better for children, and society itself will greatly improve.

It is already happening, for those who have the eyes to see it. *"The horse is out of the barn,"* as an old saying goes. There is no going back. The winds of change are blowing hard, and right before our eyes, women and men are beginning to share more in the work of the world and creating a better one, in small and big ways. You could add your own evidence to this truth, and I hope you will by sharing what you see and know on the N.E.W. website.

As we look to the future, we have the fun and challenge of imagining what kind of story we want to create for the future world as women and men become more and more fully partners everywhere, every way. Of course, if we want to create it, we need to first imagine it. All artists will tell you that they have to be able to imagine something before they can create it. That is true for all of us. Nothing new can be created without being imagined first. Therefore, it is vital that we spend time imagining what could be, as vividly and concretely as we can. What would your life be like, what would the life of this society and the world be like, if women and men were truly partners? What might our future history be like? Progress is not inevitable! We need to take responsibility for it.

Create it in your imagination, and stay with the great feelings you have when you are doing so. Imagining what could be is fun, and creative, and a first step to making it happen. We really do have the power, the real power, to create our own future story as women. And I believe Divine power is with us on this, because it is Love, and what else would love want? That Divine power works through us—through our beliefs, our faith, our determination, our actions, our imagination.

This is what I imagine:

I imagine a world in which every woman feels good about herself, and realizes and uses her innate power. She is deeply rooted in her own Divine center, her own wisdom. She is not afraid of her own power, or of the power of others. She acts with courage, imagination, and love to insure her own flourishing, and the flourishing of those around her and beyond.

I imagine a world in which every man deeply respects women and their abilities, and realizes the huge advantage of working with them as full and equal partners in the home and in society. Such men have power too—real power, power that enables the flourishing of others, and creation.

I imagine a world in which fathers and mothers share equally in the care of their house, and the care of their children. In this world of the future many women have fewer children, and those who wish are also active with men in every arena of society as full partners. Every child is wanted and treated with great love. The earth is no longer over populated, and the stress on the environment is gone.

I imagine a world in which there is no more pollution, because women and men have realized their deep connection with and dependence on the eco-system that is our planet, and are willing to live simply and in harmony with the rest of creation.

I imagine a world in which there is no more warfare, because women's skills in building relationships have been harnessed for peace, and everyone believes that above all, life is to be cherished, and violence is not an option.

I imagine a world in which resources are devoted to the welfare of all, and there are no people living in poverty and its misery. Everyone has enough to live and enjoy life.

I imagine a world in which, at every level, women are alongside men in equal numbers, creating a flourishing future in the arts, education, health, government, science, religion, and other arenas not yet invented. Since male and female energies and perspectives are finally balanced and in harmony, the societies of the world, and creation itself, reflect this balance and harmony.

Not all problems have been solved, and not everything is perfect in this future I imagine, but it is very different and much better than the present. Now, what do you imagine? What will the story of the future be as it might be written by your granddaughter, or mine?

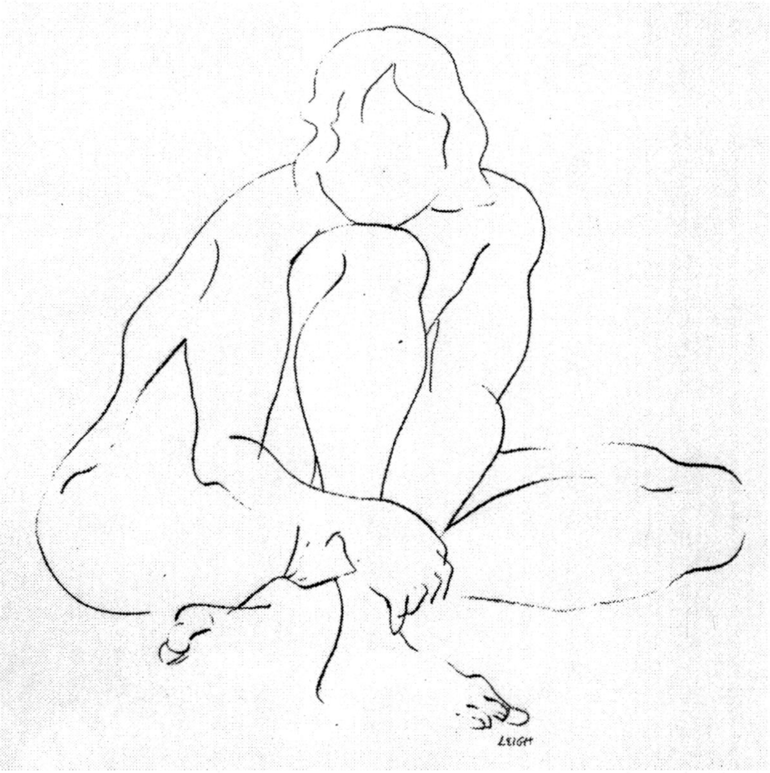
LEIGH

CHAPTER TWO

REAL POWER AND HOW TO USE IT

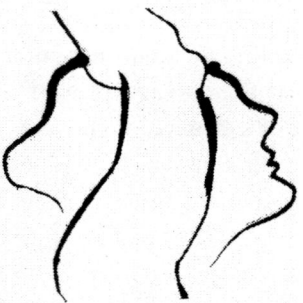

For a long time, I as a woman had a hard time accepting myself as powerful. When friends would tell me I was a powerful woman, I was not sure that was a compliment. I was unconsciously believing that power was the ability to get my way, to make things happen, whether other people liked it or not. In my mind, it was associated with force, or at least the ability to get people to accept what I wanted, because of superior status, knowledge, skills, and the ability to reward or punish those I was attempting to influence. This did not feel right to me, and so I did not want to be powerful.

Besides, it was also a very masculine thing, as I saw it, and I didn't want to "be a man." I was a woman, and I wanted to act in a way that felt fitting to me as a woman. When a certain old gentleman in the church would greet me with "Hi, chief," I would cringe. When members asked me, as senior pastor, to decide what the vision and goals of the church should be, I would protest that all of us together should decide that. I didn't like the authoritarian style by which so many churches operated, and I tried not to be trapped into it. I had a deep sense that real power was not what I generally saw being wielded in the higher echelons of the church, or other religious organizations of whatever faith, or for that matter, in government, business, and other kinds of institutions.

It seemed to me then, and still does, that power that relies on any kind of force, however subtle, is a weak strategy at the core. It depends on manipulating people with fear or rewards. By contrast, real power is the ability to help people and all of life flourish. When people or animals or plants flourish, they thrive, they prosper, and they experience the fullness of well-being. The power that helps this happen is, at its heart, profoundly creative and loving. It has nothing to do with domination, manipulation, or any sort of attempt to control others. It does have to do with the ability to create, choose, and act for the flourishing of oneself and all creation. Harry Palmer, a wise man from whose writings I have learned a great deal, says that the proper use of will power, for instance, is to control one's own attention, rather than controlling others. This kind of power, he says, is the ability to remain present and aware, and thus shape reality.

In her helpful book *Real Power*, Janet Hagberg suggests that there are stages of power that women and men grow into, or get stuck in. The earlier, immature stages are those in which people try to be powerful by association with more powerful people, by manipulation of various kinds, by threats, or by titles, position, and possessions. This includes not only money, but also knowledge not shared with others, and status symbols like the huge corner office with a view, the McMansion on the beach, and the new Mercedes.

In later, more mature stages, people act powerfully by being competent, honest, reflective, and living with integrity. They don't always "play by the rules," because they are not legalistic; but they are wise and trustworthy. They are comfortable with their own personal style, and while strong, truly listen to others and do what is best for themselves and those others. This makes them good mentors of others. They go on to be even more powerful through having a strong sense of their life's purpose, and a vision for what they want to do. They are self-accepting and accepting of others, usually calm, confident, generous in empowering others, and deeply spiritual, if not religious.

When I came to understand power in these ways, I became much more comfortable with the idea of being a powerful woman. In fact, it looked good! I believe this is what most, if not all women really want, at heart. And I believe a great many men want them to be powerful in such life-giving ways as well. I know mature men who already have and use real power, and many more who would prefer it to the kind of false power they have been taught is the prerogative of men.

There is a wonderful story, often told before weddings in certain circles, which illustrates this point. It is an old story, and some of the imagery and implications are sexist, but it makes an important point eloquently. Here it is:

Long ago, when King Arthur ruled the land, he was out riding one day when a horseman came out of the woods and attacked him, knocking him off his horse. The enemy knight was about to behead him when he realized it was the King. He thought for a second, and offered the King a reprieve from death if he could find the answer to a riddle and return in one year with the solution. The King gladly consented and asked what the riddle was.

"The riddle is, What do women want? replied the knight.

"Well, that shouldn't be impossible," answered the King. So he went back to the castle, pondering the riddle. (Stop a minute and as yourself what you think the correct answer is.)

King Arthur wasted no time in calling in Sir Gawain, one of his most trusted knights, to help him with his task. Sir Gawain was amused and quite confident that together they could find the right answer to the riddle. He set off across the land to ask all the people he could what they thought the answer to the riddle was. He went to the wisest people, the street people, the hunters, and the priests. He searched everywhere for the answer. After a year, he and the King had to admit that no single answer seemed to be the right one for the riddle.

They started off together on their journey to meet the knight, thoroughly discouraged and perplexed. As they were riding slowly along, out of the woods came an ugly witch. She had warts on her nose and walked all scrunched over, carrying a big black crooked stick. The witch saw them, stopped, and said in a scratchy voice, "I hear you are looking all over for the answer to a certain riddle."

"Yes, but we have not found it. We have given up," replied King Arthur.

"Well, I know the answer to your riddle," said the witch.

"Do tell us," commanded the king.

"Only if Sir Gawain will marry me if the answer I give you is right," replied the witch, looking directly at the knight.

"I could never ask that," replied King Arthur. " That would be like sentencing him to life in prison!"

"It's your choice," said the witch with a little smile.

At this point, Sir Gawain broke in and said, "My lord king, the choice is the possibility of your life being lost in a duel or my life being altered by marriage to this witch. There is no alternative! Allow me to marry this witch in exchange for the answer to the riddle."

"This is very hard for me. I will only go along with it if it is truly your wish and you are being honest with me," responded the King.

"Yes, this is truly what I wish," stated Gawain soberly.

King Arthur turned reluctantly towards the witch. "Very well," he muttered, "you get your terms. Now, tell us the answer to the riddle."

"I'd like to wait until we meet the knight," answered the witch, with another knowing smile.

So off they rode, the three of them each pondering a different thing in their minds. They arrived at the assigned place, and soon the knight arrived. He looked surprised that three of them were there.

"Well, King, do you have the answer to the riddle, 'What do women want?'" asked the knight.

"Yes, we think we do," offered the King, glancing at the witch.

"The answer to your riddle," proclaimed the witch triumphantly, "is simply this: women want to have rule over themselves, to have independence, and the ability to make their own choices."

"Amazing!" exclaimed the knight. "That is exactly the right answer."

King Arthur and Sir Gawain were, of course, elated that the answer was correct. They were eager to leave for home, when they realized that the witch was beaming, and it sank in. Now she was to be the wife of Sir Gawain. Refusing to dishonor themselves by breaking their word, they put her on Gawain's horse with him, and started back to the castle.

It was a glorious return. The story was told throughout the land, and there was celebrating everywhere. But soon came the time to go through with the commitment that the King and Gawain had made to the witch. Their marriage was performed right there in the castle. Sir Gawain weathered the whole thing quite well. Alas, their wedding night came, as it was bound to, and Gawain was about to perform his husbandly responsibility. Just then, the witch stopped him.

"Now, you know that I have supernatural powers," stated the witch. "Let me pose a dilemma for you on the eve of our first day of marriage: I will turn myself into a beautiful woman for you, one of the most beautiful you have ever seen. But you must make a choice. Either you can have me beautiful by day and a witch by night, or you can have me beautiful by night and a witch by day. Which will you choose?"

Sir Gawain sat back and pondered the choice for a while. Then he said with a twinkle in his eye, "I would really like for you to choose which you would most like to be, beautiful by day or by night."

The witch was so pleased with the response, she replied with the same twinkle in her eye, "Because you have given me the choice, I will choose to be beautiful and wise by day and by night."

(From Real Power, by Janet O. Hagberg)

I have a friend who I know would add to the witch's answer the word "respect." After a number of negative experiences with men, she said to me, "I just want respect! Is that too much to ask? Without that, so-called *love* just doesn't cut it."

I think she is right. And I think that one reason women don't get respect is that they don't respect themselves in many ways. Real power cannot be used without respect for oneself. This begins with respect for our bodies, as they are, not as the media tells us they should be (or anyone else!) We are feminine because we are women, by nature, and we don't need to prove it to anyone in any way. There are a thousand ways of being feminine, as the various cultures of the world reflect. Many of them in Western society are dis-empowering. For example, women have been told they had to wear certain things to be feminine, like high heels, nylons, girdles, and uncomfortable clothes that don't allow freedom of movement and action. Other cultures have their own version of feminine fashion that is restrictive. All societies are rife with stereotypes of what women should look like and how they should behave. In the West, certain stereotypes make women think they are too fat or too thin; too sexual or not sexual enough; too strong or too weak. In other cultures, the stereotypes of the way women are supposed to look and behave may be different, but often, they are not advantageous to women.

If we are to respect ourselves as women, we need to ignore any message that implies something is wrong with us because we are women. We must honor our bodies. For example our menstrual cycle and all that is associated with it should be a cause of pride, not shame. It is part of our life-giving power. Native American cultures understand this, and have special rituals to celebrate a woman's life cycle, as do some other traditional cultures. (See the book *Circle of Stones* by Judith Duerk for ways to do this.)

If we really respect our bodies, we will treat them like we would a best friend, because that is what they are—with us from the day of our birth until death do us part. Without them, we could do nothing. All we have to do is get good and sick to realize their value to us. This often happens because we drive them like slaves, ignore their needs, or feel ashamed of them. Yet, they are temples of the Divine, sacred and special. We need to feed them good food, and give them the fresh air, rest, and the exercise they need to be in their best condition. With respect, we can appreciate how our bodies look at any age, without make-up and other "beauty aids." We are beautiful, just as we are, each in our own way. If we want to decorate out bodies with make-up or jewelry, that is fine, but only out of respect and love for them, not because this is what makes us acceptable to others.

Most of all, respect for our bodies demands that we never abuse them, or allow them to be abused by others at any time. Nor should we allow it to happen to girls or women we know. The abuse of our bodies is a crime against the Divine image in us. In a huge slum in a large South

THE FUTURE FOR WOMEN - A N.E.W. BOOK

American city, the courageous women there, living in a dangerously macho culture, have adopted a wonderful way of coming to each other's aid. When a husband or any man threatens any one of them with violence, she blows her whistle, and many women drop what they are doing and come running to surround and protect her. This single brave and creative act has made a huge difference in the respect women now have in that slum. Can we do less?

Respect for our bodies, however, is inseparable from respect for our minds and souls. We need to respect what we think, what we feel, what we believe, what we choose, and our special women's perspective and wisdom, if we expect others to. How do we do this? It's easy to say, but not so easy to do, as I have discovered. One huge issue for me and most women is time, at least in our younger years. We are often so overworked, taking care of our home and families and our work outside the home, whether paid or not, that we often fail to take care of our own bodies and minds and souls.

I have certainly "been there, done that," as the saying goes. And it drained my real power. It took having my life threatened with breast cancer to make me stop and realize that I had accepted some false and damaging beliefs about myself as a woman. I had somehow gotten the idea that it was my job to take care of everybody else. But they didn't have to take care of me, and neither did I! Does that sound familiar? Without taking the time to take care of my body as I would any good friend, or my children or husband, it began to break down. Without taking enough time to carefully examine my beliefs and change them, my life was in the control of others, because my time was not my own. I not only did not have a room of my own, I didn't have enough time of my own to tend my soul, get in touch with my real self, or connect with the Divine Wisdom I believe lives in all our hearts.

Without this connection, which is the source of our real power, we are at the mercy of the Status Quo. To respect ourselves is to take the time and space we need for ourselves. We can ask those with whom we live to support us by sharing more of the work, or whatever else it takes. Everyone knows that important people's time is valuable, and we are important people—just as important as our family members or others around us.

When we do have time to ourselves, we need to spend it wisely and well. A top priority is to get in touch with the Divine Wisdom in us. We have direct access to it, by whatever name we call it, depending on our beliefs. We can listen deeply to our true feelings, our thoughts, our bodies, our dreams, and our intuition. A wise old woman taught me her way of doing this. There are many, but this one works well me and others I know of. Have a notebook and pen or pencil on hand, and in a time and place where you won't be interrupted, ask the Spirit within for guidance about your life, any problems you have, or whatever is of concern to you. Listen quietly, in a relaxed way, with closed eyes, in a prayerful or meditative attitude, and then simply write down what comes to you: words, songs, images, feelings, and hunches—whatever. Often, you will get wonderful help, and surprising too. As long as whatever comes fits with the Golden Rule that occurs in some form in all religions: "Do to others what you would want them to do for you" trust your guidance and act on it. As a double check, consult with a wise woman whose example and spiritual maturity you admire. It is true that women, like men, have their blind spots, and can rationalize selfishness or foolishness. But a strong and honest connection with the "Inner Light" or Divine Wisdom that dwells in each one of us, coupled with a commitment to the ethics of the Golden Rule (or its equivalent in other spiritual traditions) and a willingness to consult with others who are wise and loving, will help us know and live the Truth.

In our society, and in most, women have not been encouraged to trust their own truth, their own instincts, and their own ways of knowing. "Women's intuition" is often a derogatory term, when it actually refers to a great gift we have, and a source of real power. When societies do not want women to have power, they do their best to make them believe that they do not know what is best for themselves, and need to always consult others. These "others" are often male authorities, who have blind spots of their own!

Therein lies the lack of our power once again—the false and damaging beliefs that have wormed their way into our minds and hearts and shaped our lives. Every woman has her own unique set of such beliefs, and many of them are unconscious. She doesn't see them—because she is so used to having them, they are like glasses through which she looks at the world and herself.

This is why it is so important to examine our beliefs. They are the root of the problem, not men as individuals for dominating women, and not women for allowing themselves to be dominated. Neither of these would happen if people were not under the spell of damaging, false beliefs. I use the word "spell" very deliberately. Remember the spells in fairy tales and legends? They always change people or/and places into something different than their true nature. Princes are turned into frogs, or ugly beasts; princesses are shut up in towers or sleep as if dead; flourishing kingdoms become thorn-infested barren places, and so on. That is a pretty good symbolic picture of the result of the false and damaging beliefs that are at the root of the Domination System. What are some of these beliefs that hold us under a spell?

1. Women are by nature inferior to men: less strong, less intelligent, less moral, less able in a thousand ways, and most of all, not qualified to lead or govern or speak for the Divine.
2. The problems of the world are mostly the fault of women. They are not good enough mothers or wives. They first fell into sin and tempted men into sin, according to traditional interpretations of the Bible.
3. They are untrustworthy and must be controlled, sexually, and in all other ways. It is up to men to do this.
4. Men are created by God, and are inherently fit for ruling in every sphere of society. They are and should be the head of their home, and run pretty much everything else.
5. Women's sphere is in the home as bearer and raiser of children, housekeeper, and support for the husband. Education is all right. if it equips them to be better helpers to men.
6. Never should a woman have any sort of authority over a man. It is un-natural and sure to result in disaster.
7. Men have the right to have their way with women, and if necessary, may use force to do so.
8. Children are the legal possessions of their fathers, and should bear their name, but women must take most of the responsibility for raising them.
9. The earth, like women and children, is a resource for men to use as they see fit. It is all right to "conquer" mountains and space, destroy virgin forests, and pollute rivers, etc. if it serves the interests of men to do so.

10. Men are the ones who get to define what male and female nature is, and what males and females should or should not do or be.
11. It is appropriate that men decide the nature and conduct of education, science, literature, art, government, entertainment, international relations, religion, etc. In short, it is the province of men to shape culture and public life as they see fit.
12. A real man is in charge, tough, not afraid to fight (use violence), and doesn't get "sentimental"(show his feelings), A real woman is the opposite. Whatever a woman is, a man isn't, and vice-versa. In fact, the sexes are "opposite" and their relationship is a "battle of the sexes."

There are more beliefs one could list, but this is a good start. They are beliefs that are especially prevalent in western societies, but some of them are universal. Others could be added from other cultures. I put them in stark form, but they often sneak into our minds and hearts in more subtle forms. "Am I good enough? Feminine enough? Should a woman really do that?" Women in every society carry beliefs in their hearts that are hurtful and damaging to them as women.

Now the hopeful thing about all this is that the spell of such beliefs can be broken. And once that happens, everyone who is out from under the spell can begin to think, feel, and act differently. One way to break the spell that anyone can do, woman or man, is to begin to doubt what we have accepted as true, whether consciously or unconsciously. We can ask questions like "Exactly who says so? Who profits by this belief? What are its consequences?"

For example, I asked such questions of the belief I discovered was running my life. "Housework and child care is the wife's work. If she is lucky, her husband will help her out now and then. But she is made to be his help-mate, not he hers." This is what I was taught and what I saw modeled all around me from infancy on. I didn't like it, and as a teenager I would sometimes protest when my father and brothers went to do their thing after meals while Mom and we girls did the dishes. But nothing changed. I didn't have the power I do now, because a part of me back then still believed this was somehow the way it was supposed to be.

When I began seriously questioning all this as a young wife and mother, I realized that this belief benefited men far more than women. I decided I would not believe this thing I had been taught any more. I put a sign on the refrigerator that said, "The maid has moved out." I sat down with my husband and four children and said, "Here are the things around the house that have to be done. You get to choose what things you would like to do. And we'll divide up what no one wants to do. I am going to seminary, and need more time to study. Our home needs to be kept up by us as a team."

It was rough going for a while. The kids didn't always do the job they volunteered to do. And I would sabotage my own efforts for change by sometimes just doing it myself. My husband did a bit more, but ended up telling me to hire someone to come in and help with the housework because he was a busy doctor and just didn't have the time. Of course, I had to hire a woman to do the housework—a woman with far less money than we had. I couldn't have found a man to do the housework I didn't have time for, because then, and even now, housework, whether paid or unpaid, is seen in our society as "woman's work." I also saw that my husband, like most men, didn't want to spend his free time that way. He wanted to be on the golf course, or watching a good game on T.V. But all in all, as I returned over and over to my position that housework should be a team effort, I did have more time and freedom to pursue my work and interests outside the home. And all of us, because we chose to, no longer accepted the old belief about housework and childcare being the mother's sole responsibility. We experienced the truth of that saying from the African-American community: "Ain't mama happy, ain't *nobody* happy!"

This is just one small example of how important it is for us as women to examine what is going on in our lives and in our world. If it does not feel right, just, and good not only for others, but also for ourselves, we have only to ask, "What belief would produce this kind of situation?" And once you discover that, you can decide if you want to keep that belief or not.

Some beliefs are harder spells to break than others. Again, remember the fairytales? Usually, the spell is only broken by a lot of heroic effort. If we have been indoctrinated with certain beliefs we innocently accepted as children, or even as adults, because people in authority and the messages of the culture all affirmed them, we will be under their spell. If we use our innate power to question, to doubt, to disbelieve, we can free ourselves of false and damaging beliefs that keep us chained to the status quo.

In order to do this, we need to remember that it is human beings who create, and can dis-create beliefs. We do it all the time. Maybe you believed in the tooth fairy as a child. Then you doubted and finally, disbelieved. People once believed the earth was flat. Now they don't. People once believed in our country that women shouldn't be educated. Now they don't. Many white people once believed that people of other so-called colored races were inferior. Many no longer believe this. Most people once believed human beings could not fly, or go to the moon. Now they believe they can. People are perfectly capable of changing their beliefs, and they do it all the time.

The question is, which beliefs are responsible for the Domination System, and in what ways are we under their spell? Each of us, woman or man, individually, needs to ask this question over and over again, and then set about changing our beliefs. Since beliefs are a matter of mental assent to certain things we think are true, along with an emotional investment in what we believe to be true, *it takes mental and emotional detachment to undo a belief.*

One helpful tool I have discovered for doing this is by using a questioning method like the one below. I have found it very effective at loosening the hold of beliefs that keep the Domination System in place in our minds and hearts, our personal lives, and in the world at large.

The step needed first is to figure out what the belief is that underlies some situation, and question it. Let us say that I have a friend who is doing all the housework, has a full time job, and turns over all her money to her husband on demand. She is always tired, and not happy with the situation.

"Why do you do this?" I might ask.

"Because that is what a wife is supposed to do," she replies.

"Who says so?" I ask.

"My husband does—and the church I go to," she responds.

"Who benefits by this?" I ask.

"Well—it seems like my husband does the most. I don't have anything to say about how we spend our money. He gets to use it for what *he* wants.

And when he comes home from work he gets to sit and watch T.V. while I make supper and clean and take care of the kids. Yes, he definitely is the one who benefits. All I get is tired and depressed."

Now I ask a modified version of four questions used by Byron Katie in her work with people, and found in her book *Loving What Is*. Her focus is different, but the questions work in this context too.

First Question: "Is this belief that you as the wife must do all this REALLY true?" I ask. "What's the proof?"

"Well, if the church says so, it must be true, mustn't it?" she says hesitantly.

"Hasn't the church been wrong about things before?" I reply. " Like slavery? And the divine right of kings? Could it be wrong about some of the beliefs it teaches about women, seeing as how the church has been run mostly by men?"

"Maybe it isn't true after all," says my friend, a little reluctantly. It isn't easy for her to question her religious beliefs. A lot is at stake for her.

Second Question: " How does having this belief affect you? And other women? And children? And men? And society?"

It takes awhile for her to come up with the answer.

"It makes me feel resentful and unhappy," she admits. "Following it means I am exhausted most of the time. It makes me feel that my children and my husband are irresponsible and unfair to me. It feels like they don't care about me, and all I do is take care of them! I'm sure lots of other women feel the same way when they go along with this belief. And as for society—it means women are so busy just surviving, they are too tired to do things they want to do or need doing—like being an artist, or running for political office, or starting a business, or whatever."

"Exactly!" I say.

Question Three: " Can you think of a good, stress-free reason to keep this belief?"

She answers right away. "No!"

Question Four. "Who would you be without this belief? How would it feel not to have it?"

It doesn't take long for her to answer this time either—with a big smile. "I would feel such a big relief! I would feel light and free. I would feel like I could say to my husband, 'If I help you earn the money for this family, it is only fair you and the children help me take care of the household jobs. Let's sit down and figure it out. And it is also only fair that I get as much say as you do about how to spend our money. We need to plan it together. Otherwise, I won't give my money to you.'"

I recommend you use these four questions to break the spell of beliefs you may have which are damaging to women and support the Domination System.

There is more, however, to changing the Status Quo of the Domination System than dropping false and damaging beliefs. It begins there, but it doesn't end there. Positive and helpful beliefs are needed to replace the old ones in order for the kind of flourishing future we imagine to actually happen in real life. Here are some I can think of. I invite you to add your own.

1. Women's wisdom, perspective, and abilities are extremely valuable, and need to be added to those of men in order to achieve the best possible life for everyone and for creation itself.
2. Therefore, women and men need to be partners in every arena of life.
3. Men's abilities and wisdom are extremely valuable, and need to be added to those of women in the home and family on an equal basis. Children do much better with two loving parents, both equally giving them the attention and education they need.
4. Domination does not work, and is bad for people and the planet.
5. It is usually better to co-operate than compete.
6. The earth's resources need to be fairly shared and preserved, so that all have enough food and water, good health care, decent housing, and satisfying work. Women's involvement is needed in decision-making processes if this is to happen
7. Violence never solves anything in a lasting or effective way. It is not an acceptable tool for solving problems and differences.
8. Differences are good, to be respected, and never used as an excuse to rank, exclude, attack, or mistreat others in the home and in the world. Differences enrich human life, and the pooling of different perspectives makes for superior decisions.

THE FUTURE FOR WOMEN

9. No philosophies or religious beliefs that disadvantage or discriminate against any group of human beings or nature itself are worthy of acceptance or true to the Source of Truth.
10. Women have the right to define for themselves who they are, what they may do, or aspire to, and how they live their lives. Men have the same right. In co-operation and mutual respect they can learn to be true and equal partners.

Here is something interesting to try. List your beliefs about yourself, your opportunities, yourself as a spouse, parent, or worker; your role in society; you and money, you and time; and more if you like. Now, next to each belief you have listed, ask yourself, "Did I consciously choose this belief, or was I indoctrinated with it somehow? How did I come to believe this? Who or what is the source of this belief? Does this belief support fairness, equality, and my becoming the best person I can be? Do I want to keep it? Or change it?

Never underestimate the power of choosing your beliefs, and choosing beliefs that are good for you, as well as others and the world. *Our biggest contribution to a worldwide partnership society is our belief that it is possible and desirable. When enough of us choose this belief with all our hearts, it will affect the subconscious belief of the whole human family for the better. And we do have the power to choose for ourselves. No one can take that away from us. Our minds and hearts are our own. The negative indoctrination we have all received about ourselves as women in whatever society we live can be discovered and undone. Instead, we can exercise our power to follow our own inner truth, and choose what we believe.*

Never forget that we give our power away when we allow others to unduly influence what we believe. As long as we care more about what others think than about our own power, our own welfare, and our own right to choose what we believe, we will be at the mercy of others.

Some of us believe that experience is what dictates our beliefs. This belief is sure to burden us with limitations and keep us in survival mode, always reacting rather than creating new solutions for ourselves. For example, some people I know have experienced teachers who told them they couldn't sing, or couldn't draw, or were no good as athletes. They let

51

that they could or could not ...ief, we give our power away, ... are. And who created things the way they ...o ponder! The trouble is, if we believe other people ...ns are responsible for our beliefs, we become victims, ...eators.

...eve this! No matter what has happened to us, or is happening, or w... happen, we are still free to decide how to respond. The Jews who best survived the concentration camps were those who maintained this inner freedom to respond to hatred with love, and to horror with hope. We can always choose beliefs that can set us free to create a better life for ourselves and the world.

The way we experience the world and other people is determined at least as much by what we believe as by what is happening. If we are always blaming someone or something else for our experience, we can never change anything. Only when we create a different point of view, a new attitude, and fresh, helpful beliefs are we able to change ourselves or the situation. Remember my belief that I was the one mainly responsible for the housework and children? Guess what? That is what I experienced. When I changed the belief, and acted on it, my experience changed. Some of my friends once thought women could not be ministers. When they stopped believing that, they became ministers. Are there some examples you could cite to show this is true?

Our most powerful tool is our faith, which is a deep and firm conviction about our beliefs. Only strong beliefs will change our lives. In order to truly be rooted in the beliefs we chose, however, we need to repeat them over and over until they permeate our hearts and minds, just as our old, outworn beliefs were drummed into us by repetition. We need to cherish them, meditate on them, share them with others, keep developing them, protect them, and work them out in our lives. Yet, it takes even more than discarding false and damaging beliefs, and more than adopting and really believing true and helpful ones. We must be willing, as women and men who want a world of partnership, to ACT on our best beliefs. In fact, true power is the ability to do just this. When we regularly align our actions with our beliefs and intentions, we are living powerfully.

In order to do this, we need to focus and become clear about what our goals are. When we are unclear or uncertain about our goals, we tend to get in our own way, make half-hearted attempts, and in general end up acting in anything but a powerful way. There are helpful and unhelpful goals, and there are effective and ineffective ways of setting goals.

For example, some of us have multiple goals, and they contradict each other. Maybe we want to have a terrific job, but we don't want to do the work it entails. Or, we want good relationships with our loved ones, but don't want to take the time and make the necessary effort. We want to get in shape, but don't want to exercise and give up junk food. When our goals are in conflict, we create confusion, and that limits our power.

Have you ever sat down and chosen your life goals? Do you believe you can? I am talking about goals that are right for you, and chosen by you, not someone else. How do you know if a goal is right for you?

Use your best reasoning and your intuition. A goal is reasonable if you believe you can achieve it. It feels right. It excites you when you imagine it. It is life giving. Exciting. Energizing. In fact, it provides the energy for its own attainment, and more. Just imagining what it would feel like to achieve this goal will tap into your determination and courage to accomplish it.

If you have already set some goals for yourself, test them to see if they are really right for you. How do you feel when you pursue this goal? Is what you do in its pursuit enjoyable and absorbing? Is it its own reward? If a goal is not right for you, you feel it is something you have to do while waiting to get to what you want to do. You become exhausted and time drags. You feel stressed. But when you use your innate power to choose goals for your life that are right for you, the necessary energy and ideas flow to you, and your good feelings accelerate your progress towards your goals.

Here are some questions to help you choose life goals for yourself. This too is a power no one can take away from you. Use it!

1. What excites you most? What are you passionate about?
2. What would you really, really like to do?
3. Where would you like to be in one year? Three? Five? Ten?
4. If you knew you couldn't fail, what would you attempt?

5. When are you happiest?
6. What do the people you most admire do?
7. What were your goals when you were younger? A child?
8. What would you like to do, just for the heck of it?
9. What might not be impossible?

When we set goals that are truly right for us, and are for our greatest good, they will be right for the world too. Goals can give us clarity, focus, and direct our energy in a powerful way. They are a way to evoke our great creativity as women. The more they express our deepest, highest, and best desires, the more right they are for us.

Once you have chosen your goals, what YOU really want, spend time with the one or more that are top priority right now. Imagine accomplishing the goal. Let yourself FEEL how wonderful it would be—for minutes at a time—in the shower, while driving, whatever. Then ask for guidance from that inner Wisdom for what the next step is. Don't worry about the how. Just take the next step as you are guided.

You can ask the advice of others too, but in the end, always rely first and last on your own intuition, wisdom, Divine guidance—whatever you call it. Let your creativity and your gifts flower through focusing on your goals. If you run into snags, the first thing to do is ask, "What unconscious belief might be creating this snag?" Then change it and keep going.

In her book *Now It's Our Turn*, Alana Lyons gives many more ways for us as women to use our power in our relationships, at home, in the workplace, and in the world at large. Her book is full of good ideas and information as well as inspiration. She is passionate about what women can do to transform their lives and save the planet. I highly recommend it to you. Central to all these ways are two things: First is the importance of women being self-directed, independent, and making their own choices, rather than allowing what others want and think to determine the direction for their lives. Second is the importance of women banding together to accomplish their goals and act on their beliefs. Alana proposes circles of women in neighborhoods, in places of work— in all the places, in fact, where women live. Together, they can do what they cannot alone. There is great power in the united power of women. Because women live in a world with men, whether they be spouses or partners, in the home or in the workplace, in social or political settings, women need to help each other relate to men from a position of true power. Nor must women create divisions among themselves based on whether they are married or not, have children or not, are employed outside the home or not; or on racial, ethnic, or economic status. We are all in this together, and solidarity is essential.

That is why the Status Quo so often tries to divide us by keeping us so busy we have no time to get together, and by making us suspicious of and competitive with each other. When we really believe in the need for change, and the power we have as women to bring it about in our own lives and beyond, we will no longer allow ourselves to be separated from each other. It will become a top priority in our lives to unite for the purpose of empowering ourselves and all women for the sake of a better community and world. Sometimes, I would like to plaster posters everywhere saying "Women of the World! Unite! BE FREE!" I wonder what would happen?

Here is a quote I have found which summarizes the essence of what we need to do to live as the powerful women we are.

"Until one is committed, there is the chance to draw back, always creating ineffectiveness. Concerning all acts of initiative and creation, there is one elementary truth, the ignorance of which kills countless ideas and splendid plans: namely, that the moment one definitely commits oneself, then Providence moves too. All sorts of things occur to help one that would not otherwise have occurred. A whole stream of events issues from the decision, raising in one's favor all manner of unforeseen incidents and meetings and material assistance which no one would have dreamed would come their way. I have learned a deep respect for Goethe's words:

> Whatever you can do, or dream you can, begin it! Boldness has genius, magic, and power in it! (H.H. Murray from *The Scottish Himalayan Expedition.*)

I have found these words to be true in my experience.
I hope you do too.

CHAPTER THREE

THE POWER OF SACRED CIRCLES

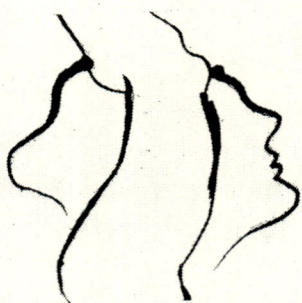

In the last chapter, I discussed how we can work to discover real power within each of us. Now I'd like to focus on how we as women can work **together** to harness our innate power. I believe gathering in sacred circles is a vital and important way to do this. I call them "sacred" because they have a special purpose and design that deeply respects and empowers each woman who participates in them. Christina Baldwin, in her book *Calling the Circle,* has this to say about the circle design.

"A circle is not just a meeting with the chairs rearranged. A circle is a way of doing things differently than we have been accustomed to. The circle is a return to our original form of community . . . rediscovering an ancient process of consultation and communion that, for tens of thousands of years had held the human community together and shaped its course . . . . familiar to us at a deeply resonant level. Over and over, people experience a sense of having been there before as they enter the circle. <u>The circle is perhaps the only way we have for most of us to get far enough outside our usual ways of acting and perceiving so that we can have a real experience of each other</u> and discover alternatives for the way things are . . . . Here power will be shared, opened up, dealt with differently, so that we may find a new way of being together." (pp. 26,29, 36, passim)

Every circle of the kind described above, including N.E.W. circles, has a sacred center. At the sacred center of these circles is the Divine Wisdom that dwells in each woman and among us when we gather together "on purpose." It is made visible by something placed at the center of the circle of gathered women. It can be as simple as a little pile of stones, a vase of flowers, a candle, or anything else desired. Usually, what is chosen fits in some way with the focus of a particular circle meeting. (More on this in Chapter Five.) Whatever is chosen represents the Divine Wisdom which is in the gathered circle, and the centering point of the circle. It is like the hub of a wheel, with the spokes radiating out to each woman.

This makes visible the truth that Divine Wisdom dwells in the sacred center of each woman, and in the sacred center of the gathered circle. To this end, every circle meeting begins with a brief centering ritual. It can be a few moments of silence as everyone takes three deep breaths, imagining Light filling themselves, each other, and the space. It can be a song, or the ringing of a bell. The various women who lead the circle by turn choose what this opening moment will be. This ritual is important, because it says, "We are now in sacred space and time. What we do and say here is important. We value this circle highly and will make the most of this precious time together."

After each woman has said her name and something about herself, and after the opening ritual, the vision and purpose for N.E.W. is read, along with the Nine Agreements that shape the circle process, and the Nine Questions that are the focus of the sharing. These initial steps are important, because they create a strong and safe container for the circle. Everyone knows what the purpose of the circle is, how the circle operates, and what the focus of each meeting is. This is especially important for newcomers, and a good reminder for everyone else as well.

The women who come always sit in a circle, because this is the wisdom we have inherited from ancient times and from the original peoples of our world. In a circle, there is no hierarchy. Everyone is equal, and everyone has something to contribute. Everything each woman says is related to the question which is the focus of that particular meeting, so there is a common issue all are exploring together which is important to the empowerment of women. A talking object is used in N.E.W. circles to assist in equal, respectful, heartfelt sharing. It can be a stone, a stick, a feather, a bowl—anything chosen by the leader for that meeting Each person gets to hold the object and speak while holding it without any kind of interruption from anyone else in the circle. Each woman is listened to silently, appreciatively, and attentively until she is done.

It is a rare and wonderful thing in our society for a woman to be listened to like this! It moves some women to tears. Often we are tuned out or interrupted as we speak. Not in N.E.W. circles! Everyone listens to each one in the circle silently, with full attention, and without judgment. When one woman is done, she passes the talking object to the woman on her right or left, or puts it in the center. There is a moment of silence between each woman's speaking, to allow what she has said to sink into the hearts of everyone. Sometimes, women in the circle will make a gesture of bringing their hands to their hearts in the silence, as a sign they have listened with their hearts and taken in lovingly whatever has been said. After everyone has had a chance to speak, the leader of the meeting will ask if anyone wants to say anything else, time permitting.

The process of the meeting described above makes possible an important principle of N.E.W. circles, which is shared leadership. Women take turns leading, so that different women in the circle have a chance to lead a meeting, choosing the opening and closing rituals and the symbols for the sacred center. This prevents the circle from becoming a pyramid, led by one leader, with everyone else following. Pyramids are not empowering for women, who all too often have been shut out of leadership in many contexts. When any willing woman leads a meeting, she is able to develop her powers of leadership as well as serve the circle in an important way. Because of the structure of N.E.W. circle meetings, special training is not necessary to be a leader. Familiarity helps, of course, but that is all. Moreover, the nature of the circle suggests that everyone in the circle is in some way responsible for honoring the process, time restraints, and everyone in the circle. This takes pressure off the leader, because she is not expected to make sure everything goes well all by herself.

In our experience with N.E.W. circles so far, the circle process described above has worked wonderfully well. It is governed by Nine Agreements, which are described below. Circle members have been most respectful of these agreements. As a result, the circles have done what they were intended to do: provide a safe and sacred space and time for women to empower themselves and each other.

Agreement One:
We meet in a circle with a sacred Center that symbolizes the Divine Wisdom within and among us.

Women cannot be truly empowered until they believe and live this truth. Circle meetings remind and encourage each woman to be and stay connected to her own sacred center, however she conceives of it. Each woman brings her own connection to Divine Wisdom to the circle. The stronger those personal connections, the stronger the circle's center is, generating great energy and insight during the meeting.

Agreement Two:
We all listen as each one speaks in turn, using a symbolic object. We do not interrupt, cross talk, or give advice during the meeting.

This is not an easy discipline to stick with, given the way most conversations and meetings take place in our society. (It is probably easier in some other societies where this way of operating is more familiar.) It is crucial to honor, however. It is easier to slip when there are only two or three women at a meeting. The informality of small numbers makes cross talk more tempting. However, it is never a good idea. Free discussion and various announcements can happen when the structured part of the meeting is over. Twelve step groups like AA as well as Native American council circles have learned the value of honoring this agreement. It makes possible a more heart felt sharing, and a feeling of safety and mutual respect.

Women in N.E.W. circles have discovered that being heard in the way this agreement prescribes is an empowering experience. Each woman's thoughts and feelings are heard and respected, and this makes it easier for them to hear and respect their own thoughts and feelings, especially in situations where this does not regularly happen. It also gives them experience in a practice they can use outside the circle to empower women they know by this kind of listening.

Agreement Three:
We honor and respect the confidentiality of what is spoken in the circle.

This agreement is vital to the ongoing welfare of N.E.W. circles and those who attend them. When confidentiality is honored, trust and honesty become possible. When it is not, trust and honesty both take a hit, and the whole circle suffers. When any one wants to tell someone outside the circle about anything said in the meeting, it is always a good idea to check first with the person you are quoting or talking about to get their approval, or speak in general terms, not using names. When in doubt, DON'T! This is where the Golden Rule applies full force: "Treat others as you want to be treated." By honoring this agreement, women can demonstrate to themselves and others that women can be trusted, and will not hurt one another by breaking confidentiality, and engaging in gossip.

Agreement Four:
We honor each one's contribution, listen without judgment, and support one another in a loving manner.

This is truly a challenge to the Status Quo! How many conversations do you remember in which this sort of courtesy was observed? What do you think would change if it came to characterize most conversations? N.E.W. circles are the place to practice this wonderful, life-giving way of hearing one another. The differences each woman brings to the circle are respected in this way. No woman goes away feeling rejected or unheard. What a great change for most women, and how empowering it is!

One helpful way to deal with the temptation to even silently judge someone is to always add the phrase after the judgmental thought, "just like me." This is based on the truth that we are mirrors of each other, and what we judge in another is often what we are blind to or repress in ourselves. Those three words "just like me" added to any judgment, tend to help us withdraw our projection, and feel compassion for the other person and ourselves. After all, every other person is learning about life, making mistakes, suffering, wanting to be happy, looking for fulfillment—"just like me." From this perspective, it is natural to support one another in a loving manner.

One marvelous example of this happened in a N.E.W. circle I attended. One of the women shared about her frustration over the poverty and seemingly impossible obstacles her minority students and their families faced in the community. She mentioned one family in particular who were out of money, out of food, out of everything, and had nowhere to turn. After the meeting ended, one woman after another quietly and unobtrusively gave her money for the family, and a couple others offered other kinds of help. She was deeply moved, and left with joy shining on her face.

Agreement Five:
We all take responsibility for the process of the circle, honoring time constraints and the agreements that guide the circle. Leadership is shared and rotated.

This way of operating is truly the most responsible and effective way to work in a group. Women have varying gifts to bring to the task of leading the circle. The whole circle benefits by the special insights and abilities each woman can offer as a leader as well as a participant. No woman has to lead, however, even though she is encouraged to do so. If she is not ready, she can wait until she is.

The leader has a special responsibility to remind people of time constraints. Depending on the allotted time for the meeting (one to two hours is the norm) and the number of women (three to nine is ideal) she can estimate about how much time each person has for sharing as the talking object is passed, leaving time for closure at the end. It helps circle members to know what their share of the time is, and it prevents having one person take so much time, there is little or none left for someone else. If this seems to be happening, it is the responsibility of the leader or anyone in the circle to gently remind the person speaking of those who have yet to speak. This is the only time interruption that is okay. Even this can be avoided if the circle decides ahead of time on some sort of time signal that catches the attention of whoever is speaking, such as a watch-timer beep, or a soft bell being struck by the leader or another person mindful of time. If there are more than nine women at a circle meeting, it is best to break up into smaller circles for the sharing part, so that everyone has a chance to speak for an adequate amount of time.

The leader and all those present at the circle meeting are also responsible for honoring all of the agreements at each meeting. If anyone feels an agreement is being ignored, she says so, and asks the circle to remember to honor it. When everyone in advance knows this is how it works, there are seldom hurt feelings or circle meetings that do not go well because some agreement is not being honored. By giving each other permission to speak out for the welfare of the group and each person in it, women learn a valuable lesson they can apply in other life situations.

At one N.E.W.circle meeting, a woman commented on what another woman was saying as she was speaking, holding the talking object. She simply held out the talking object to the woman who had interrupted her. Immediately, the woman realized she had ignored the agreement to avoid cross talk. She apologized, and fell silent so the other woman could finish what she was saying.

At the end of each meeting, someone volunteers to lead the next meeting. If this step is forgotten, when the circle next convenes, someone will need to step into leadership on the spot. This may not be as ideal, but it happens, and it can be done with the support of everyone in the circle. Shared responsibility works.

Agreement Six:
We exercise our personal right to refrain from any activity that violates

our boundaries.

This agreement empowers women by giving them permission to say "no" when they need to. It is no secret that women have often not had permission to do so. The abuse many women have suffered, often at the hands of relatives or spouses, makes this agreement especially important. Such violation of their boundaries, often at an early and vulnerable age, as well as later, makes such women especially sensitive to physical contact, for instance. Perhaps a leader suggests everyone hold hands, or that they hug each other at the end. If this, or anything else, is really uncomfortable for a woman, she is encouraged to simply not participate. Nor does she need to explain herself or defend her actions. Nothing is ever forced in N.E.W. circles. Participation in any activity is an invitation, not a requirement.

Agreement Seven:
We rely on the Wisdom of the circle's center and in each of us. The circle is like a wheel with each person connected to the hub at the center. We observe a brief silence to re-center between each person's sharing, and whenever else it is needed during the meeting.

Have you have heard the saying, "Silence is golden?" My mother used to use it at the dinner table when the four of us kids got too noisy. She was right. Words are silver, but silence is gold. It allows us to really listen to our own souls, to our own Divine Wisdom, and to the Divine Wisdom speaking through others. During N.E.W. circle meetings, it has become clear that the sharing is deeper and truer when moments of silence are observed in between each person's words. This allows the words to penetrate everyone's hearts, and provides a space that serves as a bridge to the next person's sharing.

A helpful way to enable this moment of silence is to put the talking object in the center of the circle between each person's sharing. While the talking object is in the Center, the circle is silent. Sometimes, for instance, if there is strong emotion expressed by someone, and they find it hard to continue, it helps to allow silence to hold the emotion until the person is able to continue. Silence of this sort is profoundly empowering.

One of the young women who often attends N.E.W. circles has this to say. "I think that being comfortable with silence and making space for it is very important. I love this quote: 'If we were not so single minded about keeping our lives moving, and could do nothing, perhaps a huge silence might interrupt the sadness of never understanding ourselves.'" (Pablo Neruda) When people in a circle all seek in silence for the Wisdom that is far greater than their own, new levels of understanding open up, and remarkable things happen.

Agreement Eight:
In between meetings, we may connect with each other in order to help one another continue to explore the questions of the N.E.W. process and offer support as needed. We especially reach out to those who are new to the circle meetings and process, so they feel comfortable with it.

This is an agreement, unlike the others, which has more to do with what happens outside the circle than in it. It has the potential to increase the effectiveness of the N.E.W. circles, and the process of exploration it initiates in each woman who participates. Connections can be of many kinds: phone calls, e-mails, or getting together for tea or coffee. This is especially important for women who are unable to attend N.E.W. circles as often as they would like to.

A good way to implement this agreement is to have women take a moment at the end of the meeting to choose one or two others with whom to connect between meetings. A quick exchange of phone numbers or email addresses between two women is enough to initiate some form of connection. Those who have really tried to honor this agreement have found it a most valuable thing to do. It deepens their whole experience of N.E.W. circles in empowering ways. An added benefit is that a woman who has come to a N.E.W. circle for the first time is much more likely to come back if she has a personal connection of this kind to encourage her.

Agreement Nine:
We want to reach out to as many women as possible in order to accomplish the vision of N.E.W. Therefore, we meet in a public location, safe, free of interruption, and open to any woman who wishes to attend. We encourage a small donation at the meeting to defray any expenses. The time frame can be as short as an hour once a week, or a couple of

hours once or twice a month. **We cover one of the questions at each meeting, and then repeat the cycle of Nine Questions. Ideally, there are eventually ongoing N.E.W. circles meeting in many places at many different times so that a woman can find a meeting when she wants it at a convenient time and location.**

This last agreement covers the practicalities of circle meetings. The place is important. Public places that are easy to find and accessible to anyone are necessary. Meeting in private homes, while sometimes cozier, creates many difficulties: interruptions from other family members, pets, the phone, etc. Finding the place can be a barrier. The fact that some homes are much larger and more luxurious than others can create other problems. N.E.W. circles can meet in libraries, churches, synagogues, schools, offices, etc. There are many possibilities, as long as the place is safe, free of interruption, and easy to find and access for people with disabilities. Such places are often available free, or at low cost. If there is a cost, it is a good idea to have a container in the meeting place to collect a small amount from each person to cover expenses. It is all right to have something simple for refreshment, like water, tea, juice, or coffee, but not more than that, as it becomes a distraction during the meeting and is not necessary.

The experience of N.E.W. circles so far is that it is ideal to deal with one of the Nine Questions each month. If the circle meets more than once a month, it works fine to cover the same Question more than once. Each Question covers a great deal of territory to explore, and there is no danger of too much repetition of material. In fact, experience shows that doing a Question twice or more elicits greater depth of insight.

The final part of this agreement reminds N.E.W. circle members that the purpose for which they are meeting is much bigger than any one circle. It involves reaching out to start more N.E.W. circles so that as many women as wish to have an opportunity to participate. Women who regularly attend a N.E.W. circle can see themselves as initiators of N.E.W. circles in another place or at another time.

Every N.E.W. circle meeting ends with a simple ritual chosen by the leader, such as a song, a brief silence or prayer, an inspiring quote, etc. Sometimes, before the closing ritual, if there is time, there can be one more round of sharing with the talking object, in response to the question, "Is there anything more you need or want to say?"

Finally, someone volunteers to lead the next meeting. A brief moment is taken for women to arrange for "in-between" contact, and the meeting is over. However, if some women wish to stay and continue sharing informally, this is fine, as long as women who need to leave feel free to do so at this point.

In summary, the power of sacred circles, and in particular, of N.E.W. circles, is that they are designed to take advantage of ancient universal wisdom through the circle process, and at the same time to meet contemporary needs by gathering women together to empower one another. In this way, women create a community of support for each other, so that every one can fulfill her potential and contribute in her own unique way to the larger whole. This purpose shapes everything that is done in a N.E.W. circle, and attracts women who desire to experience their true, innate power more fully so that this world becomes a better place.

Alana Lyons, in her book *Now It's Our Turn*, eloquently describes some other important reasons for women to create a community of support for each other, especially at this time in history.

"Believing our problems to be purely personal undermines our self-image and our self-confidence, and hypnotizes us into a false sense of helplessness. We come to believe that we can't control, overcome, or solve our problems, and depression sets in. But if we share our problems and our secrets as women, realizing that many situations in our lives are determined by our culture and are shared by millions of other women like ourselves, this very process encourages us to solve the problems instead of attacking and blaming ourselves. Our loneliness begins to dissolve. We begin to take positive action together . . . The success of women's circles lies in the fact that most women find it more inspiring to reach for a dream with someone else. We know how to work diligently for others; in fact, we often work harder for others than we do for ourselves." (p. 12, 122-124, passim)

I would add that as we begin to work diligently for each other and ourselves for a change, great and good things are bound to happen! By joining together in circles that empower us, we will find that we reach our potential far more quickly. And the whole world will benefit. Think what could happen if there were circles of women, meeting deliberately to empower each other, and make positive change, in every home, school, office, corporation, religious institution, government office, neighborhood, and so on! Think how such circles would help us as women network, negotiate with people in power, change our environments, and make a difference for the next generation. There is enormous, as yet unleashed power in the deliberate, regular gathering of women together in such circles. In fact, it is unlikely that the Status Quo will change unless women gather in sacred circles, and thereby find the courage, inspiration, and support to insist that they be treated as equal partners in their homes and in the world.

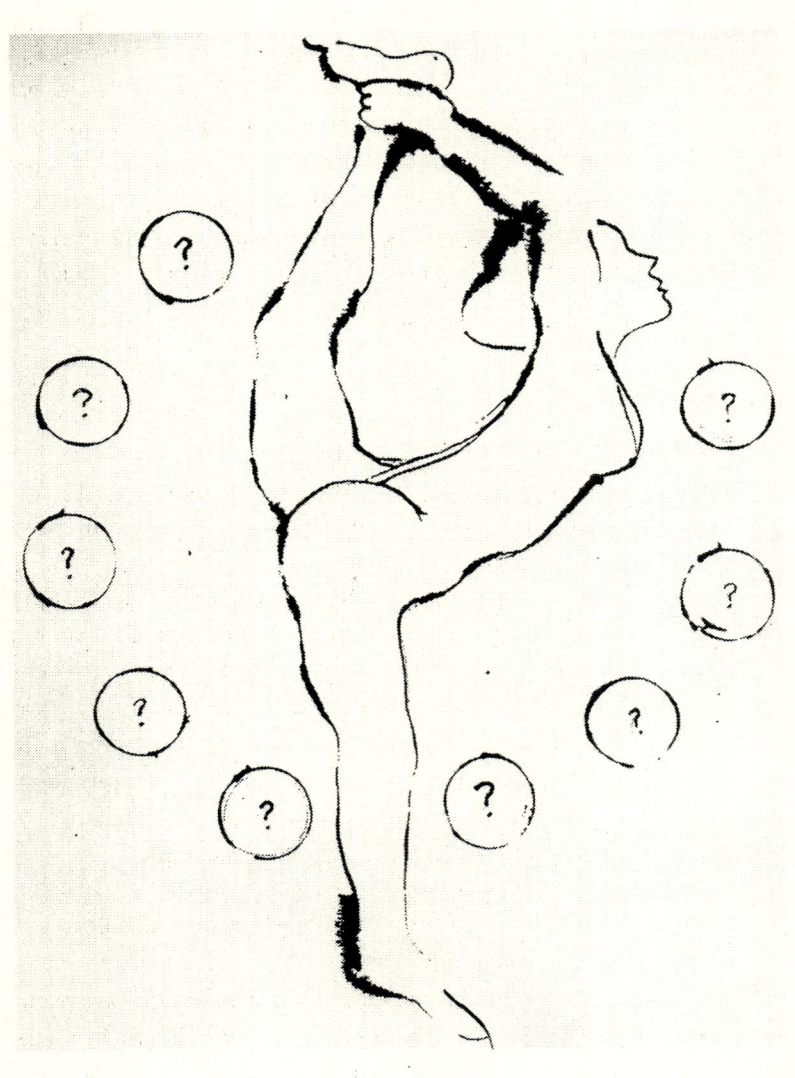

CHAPTER FOUR

THE POWER OF QUESTIONING

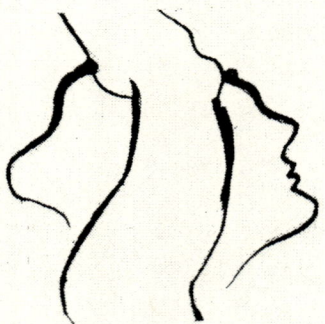

Have you ever pondered how powerful the process of questioning is? Questions, unlike answers, are open-ended, allowing for exploring and learning. Answers, even satisfying ones, can close the doors, and contribute to a false sense of security or even smugness. People who "know all the answers" are seldom appreciated. Many of us sense instinctively that no one and no group has all the answers. Those who claim they do often have a certain air of superiority and self-righteousness that is most unattractive. The Truth is so huge, so mysterious, that the most brilliant people and belief systems can only catch glimpses of it.

The story of the blind men and the elephant reveals this in a vivid and funny way. Several blind men are gathered around an elephant. One feels its trunk and proclaims that an elephant is very much like a snake. Another feels its massive side and proclaims it is more like a wall. Another feels its leg and proclaims it is like a pillar. And so on. Of course, they are all wrong, and all right. They are closest to the truth when they put all their individual truths together. But when they each proclaim, "I know what an elephant is like. It's the way I perceive it," it is laughable. How much better if each one said, "This is what I am sensing is true about an elephant. But maybe there's more. I wonder what it is? What, my friend, do you perceive?"

Such questions keep the questioner open and connected to what additional truth he or she has yet to discover. Great teachers have known this for a long time, in whatever cultures they lived. Socrates, one of the greatest thinkers of the Western world, always asked questions as his teaching method. His view was that questions brought out what a person already knew deep down. The very word "education" means, "to draw out." That is what questions do.

A certain famous rabbi was once asked by an irate student who wanted more answers, "Rabbi, why is it that every time we ask you a question, you answer with another question?" The Rabbi replied with a twinkle in his eye, "So—what's wrong with questions?" A good question!

Children ask questions because they are so eager to explore their world. Maybe we give them too many answers too soon, instead of just encouraging them to ask more questions. The rabbi's approach can work well, and take the pressure off us adults to have the answers. Children can ask very big and hard-to-answer questions. Just ask them a question in return!

Most people ask questions as a way of finding out more about something or someone, unless their questions are disguised opinions. Some questions challenge conventional wisdom and our own assumptions and beliefs. In a way, they can be threatening when used this way. The powers-that-be don't like questions that challenge the Status Quo. Many people don't like questions that either make them realize they just don't know something, or that they have assumptions that might not be true or helpful. One of these is the usually unconscious assumption that they need to know the answers, or need to be "right" about what they think or believe. School systems certainly reinforce this by punishing those who don't have the answers, or have the wrong ones. When this experience spills over into everyday life, it creates a lot of insecurity for people.

It takes courage to ask questions—at least certain questions. But it is important to ask them. One of the women who comes often to N.E.W. circles has attended twelve-step groups for quite awhile. This is her experience, in her own words:

"I came across this quote. '*We see ourselves as broken, and then set out on a long and frustrating journey to fill our emptiness. But it is not fixing that we require, it is awakening.*' (Alan Cohen) It brought to mind the difference I see between typical twelve-step work and the N.E.W. circle process. The twelve steps talk about a spiritual awakening, but only after a process of admitting our wrongs, listing our shortcomings, and asking Godde to remove our defects of character. In the circle process, we simply ask questions. This creates awareness and awakening."

That has certainly been our experience in N.E.W. circles. We do not use steps, because they are givens that state how things are and what must be done. Questions are more open-ended, and therefore more empowering for us as women. We have been told all too often how it is and what we must do. We have not been encouraged to ask the kind of questions that *challenge* "how it is" and "what we must do!" Questions enable us to explore our own inner wisdom, the truth of our own personal experience, and the beliefs that are shaping our lives. There are no "wrong answers," no "steps you must take." By asking questions, we are able to break the hold of assumptions that are crippling our lives and robbing us of power.

Not all questions, of course, are equally helpful. Asking the right question at the right time is an art each of us can learn with great benefit. The Nine Questions that are the heart of the N.E.W. circle process have been carefully chosen and placed in a certain order so that by asking them, we can use the questions as a key to open one door after another into the free space of empowered living. They are the distillation of the experience of countless women who, by asking these questions in one form or another, have discovered how to realize and use their wonderful, life-giving, innate power.

These are the Nine Questions, with an explanation of what door each one opens, what kind of power it opens into, and what some women have discovered by using these questions as keys to their own empowerment.

Question One:
What am I grateful to have survived and accomplished?
Who or what has empowered me in my life so far?

As a human being, you have survived many obstacles and hurts just to make it to where you are today. If you are a woman, you have a special set of obstacles and hurts you have survived. All over the world, you are much more likely than men to have been abused sexually, physically, or emotionally. You have had to overcome negative attitudes and obstacles because of your gender.

If you see yourself as a survivor of whatever difficulties you have lived through, you can realize the strength it took to get through them. Instead of being dis-empowered by a victim mentality (poor me) you are empowered by seeing your strength, and by realizing the help you may have had, human and Divine. Since you made it through this far, you can make it through the future, whatever comes your way. You will have what it takes, including human and Divine support. That is an empowering belief! It lets you look at the past with pride and gratitude, and the future with faith and hope. Feeling like a victim is like being in a cage. This first part of the question opens the door so you can walk out into a space in which you are a victor rather than a victim.

The second part of the question unlocks the door of the cage of false humility. As a woman, you have probably been encouraged to be humble, which often means not taking credit for what you have accomplished, but giving it to someone else. History, now that we are starting to see the "herstory" side of it, is full of examples in which men got the credit for what women actually did. For instance, I was always taught that William Booth founded the Salvation Army. It turns out that his wife, Catherine, was at least as, if not more influential in its founding. Recently, I heard a lecture in which Frank Lloyd Wright was given credit for creating the famous Chapel of the Holy Cross in Sedona, when it was actually a woman architect's genius that was behind it. You could probably cite some examples of this yourself.

This question gives you the key to recognizing what you have accomplished. Many women don't see running a household and raising children, or being a waitress, or creating a garden, as an accomplishment worth noting. But these things are. True, our society does not value women's work in the home. In France, by contrast, women get social security for the years spent taking care of home and family. That is an important way to honor the work women do in the private sector. In this country, "pink collar" jobs are always paid less and women who give the best years of their lives to raising a family get no financial security for it. But the value of what we do is not measured by money. What we do as women keeps the whole world going. Without us, it would come to a screeching halt. What if all women just didn't do anything on August 26, Women's Equality Day, every year. Can you imagine the impact?

Look at your life, and give yourself credit for the big or small things you have accomplished with your own labor, your own ideas, your own creativity, and your own love. List those accomplishments. Then be grateful in the way that best expresses your beliefs and your feelings. True humility is gratefully and realistically recognizing the gifts you have been given and how you have used them. Let us also make sure credit and recognition is given to one another. If society ignores our accomplishments, we certainly do not have to!

This second part of the question opens the door into a space in which you stand tall and proud of yourself as a woman because of who you are and what you have accomplished. If you value what you have done, it is more likely that others will. Even if they do not, at least you can give yourself the benefit of self-appreciation. You need no longer hide your light under a bushel, as an old Sunday school song puts it. Doesn't it feel better to be out from under that bushel of false humility? Try it. Take it off yourself, and take it off other women and girls!

The third part of the question opens the door of the cage of feeling like it is all up to you. When you realize all the people, both women and men, who have empowered you, then your heart opens up with gratitude. You see the past with new eyes, and yourself too. When you realize the experiences of the past that have empowered you, you have a clearer picture of how they could continue to bear fruit now and in your future. For example, when I was a girl, I was empowered by being on the track team and being a really fast runner and high jumper. I can't run that fast or jump that high any more, but I have found that physical movement, and pushing my limits a little as I walk, dance, or ski, gives me that same powerful exhilaration I enjoyed as a girl.

When we considered this question in our N.E.W. circles, we had a pile of stones in a bowl at the center of the circle. We invited each woman, after she spoke, to come to the center, take one of the stones, and put it on the table (or the cloth on the floor at the center) and tell about people who had empowered her. Some talked about grandmothers, some about fathers, some about friends, some about mothers, some about teachers or neighbors. A common thread was the way that women had felt empowered by seeing other women living their lives in a powerful way, doing what they really wanted, overcoming obstacles, etc. This part of the question unlocks the door to the space in which women are empowered by one another in an intentional way, and are recognized for doing so.

Question Two:
What damaging, false beliefs about myself and/or women do I want to release? What healing, helpful beliefs do I want to affirm and live?

The first part of this question may take some courage and digging to answer. We have talked in an earlier chapter in this book about beliefs, how greatly they shape our lives, and how hard it can be to see some of them, because they are transparent—we look right through them. If you are experiencing anything in your life that you would like to be different, ask what belief you might have that would contribute to that experience. Look particularly at what false, damaging beliefs about yourself or women in general you might have.

For example, there was a time in my life when I actually preferred the company of men to women. I thought women were shallower, more gossipy, didn't talk about ideas like men did, were too caught up in the trivial, and were just less interesting. Eventually, I came to realize how untrue this belief was, and how damaging it was to the possibility of friendship with other women. I now count women as my best friends, and enjoy their company more than the company of many men.

There is plenty of material in our society to work on when it comes to false and damaging beliefs about women! It is most important to see which ones affect you personally, but also to consider how you may be unconsciously harboring some of these same negative beliefs about women in general yourself. Take a good, hard look. This question opens the door from the cage of negative self-esteem, and crippled functioning in life, into the space of knowing that what you thought was reality was just a belief, and can be changed if you choose too. This is the powerful space of self-determination, rather than being caged in by the beliefs of others around you.

The second part of this question opens the door into that wonderful space where you get to be the creator of what you believe about yourself and other women. Since that is your innate power, what do you want, what do you choose to believe? What are the very best, greatest beliefs you can imagine about who you are and what you can do and be? About what other women are and can do and be? You have the power to choose. Use that power fully.

If it helps, go back and review the chapter on Real Power, and the list of false, damaging beliefs, and true, helpful beliefs. Then create your own positive beliefs, and live them. Remind yourself of them often. Put them on your mirror or wall or door. Do whatever you can to use this question as a key to the power that is yours as a creative woman, choosing for yourself what you believe.

When we considered this question in our N.E.W. circles, a common thread in our answers to what false, damaging beliefs we wanted to release was some form of "I am not good enough in some way. I don't measure up to expectations." To release these and other false beliefs, we had a fire-proof bowl in the center of the circle. Then we wrote those negative beliefs down, and burned them in the bowl, so they turned to smoke and ashes.

When we talked about the positive, helpful beliefs we wanted to affirm, we each put a flower in a vase to symbolize the flowering of our chosen beliefs in our life. Together, they made a bouquet representing how women can blossom when they believe what is good and true and inspiring about one another as well as themselves.

For me personally, the belief that helps me with all this is that we are fully images or representatives of the Divine. Our true nature is good. It may be covered over by layers of false beliefs that produce negative attitudes and actions, but underneath, we are all jewels. This question helps us scrape off those layers of crud so we can shine in all our glory! The Grace-full truth about our true selves can shine out, reflected to us by those around us who see this truth.

Question Three:
How have I found and followed my own inner authority? How shall I continue to do so?

Do you believe that you have your own authority? That it is divinely given, and is within you, rather than residing in some other person or institution? Again, it is a matter of belief. For instance, if you genuinely recognize some sacred scripture as having authority for you, it is because you have personally experienced that it resonates with your own sense of what is right, good, and true. If you recognize something or someone as having authority over you just because you have been told that it does, then you are giving your power away. Organized religion, unfortunately, in spite of its many benefits, has been a chief culprit in trying to rob women of their innate inner authority to believe as they choose to.

The United States was founded on a belief in the sacred "freedom of conscience," as was the whole Protestant church. Yet, women have been told by various religions what they must believe, and that they are always to defer to religious authorities, who have usually been men. They, in turn, have told women to defer to the authority of the men in their lives, husbands most especially, but others as well. What do you, as a free woman, not a slave, choose to believe?

I have a good woman friend, a Muslim, who has had the courage to claim her own inner authority in the face of edicts issued by authorities in her faith about the nature and place of women. She has withstood attack and suffered alienation from people in her faith community, but she will not give her power away. I have good friends from strict evangelical Christian backgrounds who have done the same thing. Because religion and culture are so closely intertwined, we as women find we are often not only up against religious claims to final authority, but cultural claims as well. It takes a lot of strength for us to stand firm on the ground of our own right to choose what we believe, and to hold to our own inner authority about what is right, true, and good for us and others. Women in every country and culture have this challenge.

By affirming our right and need to interpret sacred texts and traditions for ourselves, we are not attacking religion or Divine authority per se. We are simply insisting on our own interpretive authority, the same authority men have claimed for themselves. We are saying that women as well as men have direct, unmediated access to the Divine, and that we will not allow ourselves to be limited, defined, and marginalized by one-sided male interpretations of religious truth. Once we decide to take up the challenge, the question is "how?"

To begin with, we must believe that the source of our own spiritual authority is within us—our hearts, our minds, our souls, and our spirits. There, a Divine spark shines. Christians call it the Holy Spirit, or Christ within. Buddhists call it Buddha nature. Hindus call it Atman. Taoists call it the Tao. Jews call it the Shekinah. I like to call it Divine Wisdom. Choose what speaks best to you, but realize that you are the temple, the sanctuary of the Holy One. And you have direct access to that One, through prayer, meditation, silent listening, and other spiritual practices. Through that direct access, we can personally know the Truth that sets us free.

When we shared how we discovered and follow our own Inner Authority in our N.E.W. circles, a common thread was "time alone." If we allow ourselves to be robbed of time to connect with our souls, we will lose the source of our power. It can be a few minutes at the start or end of the day, or in between. In fact, connecting daily for short periods frequently as we do other things, like bathe, walk, wash dishes, cook, drive, and so on is always possible. We can turn our active life into a silent tuning in to the Divine within. And we need to claim "Sabbaths," or regular longer times weekly, monthly, and yearly in which to listen more fully to Divine Wisdom and Guidance. The place and time will differ with every woman. But we must not let ourselves be robbed of connection with the source of our power by giving in to the pressure of the multiple demands on many of our lives.

We must simply make the time, claim for ourselves the time, to consult our own inner Authority to guide our decisions about what to believe, what to do or not do—in short, how to live. Otherwise, we will be guided unconsciously by our programming and the society around us. It will be far harder to resist the pressure of outer authority.

We need to help each other with this. What sort of help from another woman would enable you to take this kind of time to focus on your inner Wisdom? What could you do for another woman to help her do the same? I have friends who, with enormous dedication, have created safe, wonderful retreat centers where women can go for a day or longer, to commune with their souls. (Some are listed in the Resource Appendix.) Those of us who are living in homes that are empty during the day can offer such space to each other. There is always the great outdoors. Somehow, being in a place where we are not responsible for doing things really helps most of us. Once we make time for this crucial connection a top priority in our lives, we can find a way and a place to do it. My mother always said, "Where there is a will, there is a way."

Often, spiritual friendships can be of great help in finding and following our own inner spiritual authority. Do you know a wise, spiritual woman who you can sense has already been doing this for a good while? Ask her if she will meet with you so you can get the support you need to be true to your own truth and vision. Even if you regularly tune in to your own inner Wisdom, you may find that it is hard to follow it when it leads you to "swim upstream" against the flow of the social circles in which you live. I certainly experienced this when I felt "called" to be a minister back in the 'seventies.

My Muslim friend continues to experience this as she feels led to spiritual leadership in her community. You may have also experienced this in your own unique way, or know friends who have. If they have the courage and stamina to follow their own authority and do what their soul leads them to do, ask them how, and get support from them for doing the same thing yourself.

When you are challenged about your inner authority, and made to feel you must describe or prove it, resist the temptation to do so, unless you feel strong and self-confident, or Divinely led to do so. You don't have to prove anything to anyone. You simply choose to believe that it is best for you to follow your own spiritual authority, and that is all you need to say. You are a free woman, and a good one. Others don't have to agree with you. But they do not have the right to try to stop you from finding and following your own spiritual authority. They can quote this or that tradition or scripture, but stand fast in your own divine Center. Remember, religious traditions are clad in male garments, and so are their scriptures. This means that the religious truth they represent is one-sided, filtered through the lenses of only half the human race.

As women, we have the right to question its authority over our lives, and to decide for ourselves what we choose to believe and follow from those traditions, and what we do not. If you are labeled a "bad Christian, or Muslim, or Buddhist" or whatever, let it roll off you like water off a duck's back. The label is just another person's opinion, not the Eternal Truth, even if they say it is. Let no one separate you from the truth of your own spiritual authority. Discover your own unique way to find and follow it, whatever happens. Then you can unlock the cage of external authority, and fly on the free wings of the Spirit.

There are many ways women have pioneered ways to help connect with and follow their own inner authority. Some books that describe what they have discovered are listed in the Resource Appendix. I have already mentioned the method of laying aside one's own mind chatter, and listening for specific Divine guidance with a notebook and pen or pencil in hand, and writing down what comes.

Another way was taught to me by a friend who is from the Native American tradition. Take a few deep breaths with your eyes closed (in a place you won't be interrupted.) Then imagine yourself in a beautiful, safe place. Use all your senses to get a strong, clear feeling for what it is like. Then, prayerfully, ask for Divine Guidance to come to you in some form you can best relate to at this time in your life. It could be a wise old woman or man, a wise little child, an animal, an angel, or whatever. Ask that figure of Wisdom to guide you, realizing that what comes to your imagination is guided by the Divine. You can test the guidance given you by your own highest ethical standards and your inner sense of rightness and truth. You can also ask for an outer "sign" of confirmation. I know many people who find this the way that works best for them.

The important thing is that you find a way to tune in to your inner authority that works for you, and that you follow it, preferably with the support of at least one or more other women who are experienced and whose lives show the good fruit of such a practice.

In short, as long as you believe you do not have the right or the power to claim your own spiritual authority as a woman by choosing what to believe and living by it, you cannot live in an empowered way. You will always be shackled by the chains of the beliefs of others in your religion, your culture, and your social circles. It is your choice. You can live in the cage of others' beliefs, (often unconsciously,) or you can consciously fly on your own. It might seem safer and easier to sit in that cage, but that is not being true to your nature. You were meant to fly into the sky of the boundless possibilities that open up to you once you use your innate spiritual power to choose for yourself.

Question Four:
What are the spiritual practices and resources that most empower me?

This question builds on the last, and assumes that you as a woman believe you are most empowered when you find and follow your own Divine Inner Authority, however that is named and conceived. There are many ways to do this, and a couple of them have already been suggested above.

This question helps you search your own heart and life and look at what your spiritual practice has been and is and might be, through the lens of what has most empowered you, and what might most empower you in the future.

Naturally, every single woman answers this one differently. Sometimes, the answers are quite surprising, and lead to new insights, and further questions. As you ponder this question for yourself, ask yourself when, in the past, you felt closest to Godde, in whatever way you conceive of the Divine. Was it out in nature? That is an answer many, many women give. We have a very natural, deep connection to earth. Was it while gardening? Sitting as a girl in a secret hiding place? Walking on the beach or through a meadow? Was it while listening to music? Dancing? Singing? Having a heart to heart conversation with a friend? Drawing something? Cooking? Creating something? Birthing and nursing a baby? Caring for someone sick? Reading? Writing? The questions, and their answers, could go on and on. Many things you have experienced as spiritual, or opening you to the Divine, you may not have considered a spiritual practice. I believe that any way you find and choose for yourself to open your mind and heart to Godde is a spiritual practice.

For instance, these days I often feel closest to Godde when I am walking in nature, when I am holding or playing with a child, or when I am playing with clay or painting. Insights come to me, shifts in attitude that are positive, hunches, and above all, a sense of living in a Divine, Loving embrace. There was a time when reading spiritual words, singing spiritual songs, and listening to my dreams were the ways I felt closest to Godde. How about you?

When I suggest looking through the "empowerment" lens at this question, what I mean is simply, what gives you the strongest sense of connection to the Divine? What gives you the greatest inner clarity and assurance when it comes to knowing what to do or say, and how to live?

Sometimes it is obvious. Often, it is subtle, and takes some deep reflection. But it is worth the effort to discover the answer to this question for yourself, because it will help you sustain that all—important connection to your Divine Source, and live according to its Wisdom. Just as we cannot become good at a sport, or music, or art, without practice, neither can we become good at connecting with and following our Inner Wisdom or soul, without spiritual practices that really work for us.

When we explored this question in our N.E.W. circles, we planted seeds in a pot of soil as symbols of the practices we wanted to plant in the soil of our souls so they would bear fruit in our lives. We were inspired by the choices we heard each other making, and they often sparked a deeper insight into what each of us wanted to choose as our spiritual practices at this time in our lives.

Generally, women are imbedded in the daily responsibilities of life, and are most helped by spiritual practices they can weave into their lives as they are. So when you look for what will work best for you, be realistic. What, in your daily round of activities, can you turn into prayer, into connection with the Spirit? For example, a shower or bath could become a prayer of immersion in the waters of Divine Love. Eating could be a means of holy communion with the Source of all goodness. Walking could be an extended prayer of thanksgiving and praise. How could other things you normally do become prayer-full? When you need guidance, how could you tune in more to your intuition, or sense of what is really going on, and know how to respond? Keep asking these questions, and you will find the answers for yourself. Remember—don't try to do what you can't do. Do what you can! You will be guided if you ask for it. And you will find your spiritual practices the source of your greatest and truest power.

Question Five:
What obstacles to using my innate power as a woman have I/we encountered? What are some strategies for dealing with them? How do I/we stop giving away my/our power?

This question has a lot in it. It comes at this point, because the first four questions have really been centered on your personal and inner life. The inner work (or play, if you prefer!) of examining your beliefs; discarding damaging ones and choosing helpful ones; focusing on your own inner authority, and the spiritual practices and resources that will help you make the spiritual dimension central in your life—all of these get you ready for this question. In a way, it is a bridge between the very personal and inner focus of the first questions, and the more outward focus of those that come after it.

There are some obstacles that you might have encountered as a woman that are unique to you and your life situation. What might those be? In our N.E.W. circles, we discovered that most of the obstacles we talked about were familiar to us. The most common obstacle, we discovered, was inside us: the fear that kept us from naming and claiming our true power. Some women feared damaging or even breaking up their marriages if they did so. Others feared losing their jobs. Still others feared losing friends, or the acceptance of their community, especially their religious community. The fear was a response to the obstacles of opposition.

I believe there is a good reason for this fear we all experience when we consider the kinds of changes we have been talking about in this book. We have a very deep memory, as women, of the terrible things we have suffered over the centuries: rape, abuse, sexual slavery, being burned and tortured as witches, being stoned for sins against religious rules, denial of education and any kind of economic independence, and so on and on. In our collective unconscious, these things still live, and affect us as women consciously and unconsciously.

We are like the princess in the famous legend of St. George and the Dragon. At some level, many of us feel tied up and guarded by the fearsome Dragon of Domination, who is not about to let us go! In fact, our lives are constantly in danger as prisoners of this Dragon. No wonder we are afraid when we think of challenging this huge system we live in!

Now legends last because they tell an inner truth, not just an interesting story about once upon a time. One possible meaning of this legend of St. George and the Dragon for our time is this: Our feminine side has been tied up and rendered helpless. We don't like fighting, we can't see a way out, and we are reduced to helplessness when our focus is on the Dragon—all the obstacles that keep us from being powerful women in this world. It's much worse for some of us than others, but we all are familiar with this situation.

In the story, a very brave, strong, good man finally volunteers to fight the dragon. Many others have tried and failed, but he is determined, because deep down he believes he can defeat the dragon. And he does, after a terrific battle. The old way of seeing this story was to reinforce how helpless women are unless the right man comes along and rescues her. The new way of seeing this story is to identify St. George as the strong, brave part of us. As women, we too have that part of us that is willing to fight, willing to take risks, and face up to the dragon, whatever it is, believing it is possible to overcome it.

You can be like St. George, or, if you like, St. Joan of Arc, or Deborah, the famous judge and military leader whose story is in the Bible—or any other brave woman you know of who fought against great odds to do what she knew was necessary and right, and won. I think of a woman named Riffat Hassan, for example, who at great risk and with enormous courage, is fighting to help stop violence against women in Pakistan, including the jailing and even killing of women who are raped. I think also of the women who won women in the United States the right to vote.

They suffered the full force of the religious and political establishment of their day against them. They were taunted, harassed, even jailed. Women in South American, the Middle East, and other countries still suffer this kind of treatment when they fight for their rights.

Have you or I suffered such indignities? Most of us have not. Are we willing to suffer and take great risks, if we have to, for the sake of our daughters and granddaughters, nieces, and young friends? Men have been willing to go to war and be killed to protect their loved ones and their land. We can draw on that same courage to face the difficulties of doing what we need to in our efforts to live as powerful women. The welfare of our society and the whole world depends on it. Men cannot and will not change the Status Quo on their own. True, there are and will be good men, like St. George, who will come to our aid, at least sometimes. But in the end, it is up to you and me, in our lifetime, to make the changes that must be made.

Once you are clear about the inner and outer obstacles you still face as a woman, what then? The second part of the question asks you to consider what strategies might work for dealing with those obstacles. As we talked about this in our N.E.W. circles, we discovered a number that have worked well for many women, and they might work well for you. One strategy that is low-risk and can be done by anyone is to "defect in place." You stay where you are—in your job or religious community, home, or wherever, but you don't give your mental assent to what is going on that you see is not right for you and/or women in general. You find subtle ways to resist.

For instance, if you are afraid to insist that your husband and children (if any) take a fair share of the housework, you can just not do certain things, or not do them well. Cook lousy meals. Let the dirty laundry lie there. Don't make the beds. If anyone complains, you can offer the opportunity to do those things themselves, and do them well. It's kind of like the way the Danish workers slowed down and got really ineffective under Nazi occupation. It wasn't too obvious, but it was enough to make sure the oppressive system of foreign occupation did not function very well. My father had a good way of summarizing a strategy to get out of doing something you choose not to do. "Be willing, but awkward." Sometimes not doing a good job can be an effective strategy!

Here is another approach. In your work place, you could get a few women together to start a circle to empower each other and work for changes you would like to see. The same strategy could work in schools or neighborhoods or religious institutions. As determined and dedicated circles of women you could meet to support each other in pushing for the changes you choose. There is enormous power in such solidarity. United we stand, divided we fall! Jean Shinoda Bolen's book *The Millionth Circle* makes an eloquent case for this approach, as does *Now It's Our Turn* by Alana Lyons. The latter book gives specific strategies to try, especially in the work place.

There are higher risk strategies that work well too. I sometimes imagine a million nursing mothers staging a sit-in at the Pentagon, with perhaps a good supply of grandmothers along as well, refusing to move until there is a pledge to put as much money and personnel into peace and conflict resolution as is now put into weaponry and training for war. Try to imagine other strategies that could work in bringing about the changes that are needed. Find out what other women around the world are doing, and what they have done in the past to bring about change. For instance, there is a famous Greek play about women who refused to have sex with their husbands until they stopped going to war. Recently, in the newly elected government gatherings in Afghanistan, women refused to be quiet when told to by men, and instead insisted that they have influential positions in government, and that the government do something about the terrible plight of women and girls in their country. They succeeded in overcoming the resistance of many of the men, and getting at least some of what they wanted! They just wouldn't do what they were told to do. And it worked.

Still another strategy is economic. We may not make as much as men do, but we as women have huge economic power. We spend a lot of money as a group. Why not use our dollars to support companies and causes that give women a fair deal and act according to our ethical standards, and simply refuse to buy from those who don't care for the environment or women or minorities and make profit their sole motive. If we women went on a weeklong buying strike and just didn't spend anything for those seven days, we would make clear what economic power we have.

The advantage of talking about strategies after thinking about obstacles is that doing so reinforces the belief that "we can overcome." There is a way. It's not if, but when and how. That is an approach that empowers us as women. We don't give up. We don't give in. We do give ourselves permission to resist, persist, and make change happen. As you consider and try strategies of your own for overcoming the obstacles you face, visit the N.E.W. website and share what you have done so others can benefit from it.

The third part of this question assumes that you, as a woman, have given your power away, and probably still do, in some way or other. Here are some ways we shared in our N.E.W. circles.

1. You and I give our power away when we think we have to take care of everyone else. This keeps us from realizing what our own needs and abilities are, and using them in a fitting way in the world.
2. We give our power away when we do not say what we need to say in a situation that does not feel good to us.
3. We give our power away when we try to always make peace and avoid conflict. Some conflict, if done in a fair and honest way, can be beneficial to all the parties concerned. It is better than sweeping things under the rug.
4. We give our power away when we let ourselves get so busy we have no time for ourselves and connecting with our souls.
5. We give our power away when we accept stereotypes and traditional roles without questioning them.

I know you can think of many more ways you and women in general give away their power. Once we know how we do this, we can stop doing it.

Having the support of at least a few other women really helps in this effort. That is why N.E.W. circles are so important. Until you start one yourself, or find one near you, at least hook up with a friend or two and help each other strategize on how to overcome obstacles and not give your power away. Doing this three-fold question can open the door into a whole new realm of possibilities for the use of your innate power. So go through that door, leap over those obstacles, and run free!

Question Six:
What can I imagine, and what do I want for my flourishing, and the flourishing of all?

The reason for this question is that it is difficult, if not impossible, for us as women to create the future we want if we do not first imagine it. Exploring this question is sort of like making a blueprint for a building.

In her book *Excuse Me, Your Life is Waiting: the astonishing power of feelings*, Lynn Grabhorn has some very interesting things to say about how this works.

Modern day physicists have finally come to agree that energy and matter are one and the same . . . everything vibrates, because everything is energy. Pure, pulsing, ever-flowing energy. . . . . So whether it's high vibrational joy energy, or low vibrational worry energy, what we're vibrationally offering in any moment is what we're attracting back. We are the initiators of the vibrations, therefore the magnets. We may be flesh and blood, but first and foremost we are energy—magnetic energy, at that! Which makes us living, breathing magnets. (p. 12)

Because we exist on this planet in a predominantly low frequency field of energy born of over six billion people who are vibrating more feelings of stress and fearfulness than joy, we involuntarily take in those vibrations and react to them. Which means that until we consciously learn to override the pervasive low frequencies in which we exist, we will keep attracting unpleasant outcomes into our lives day after tiresome day . . . . There's just no way around it; the way we feel is the way we attract. We get what we emotionally focus on! Focus on what we want with passion and excitement, and presto! It's on its way. Focus on what we don't want with the same passion (such as worry, concern, etc.) and presto! It too will be on its way. (p.18)

You never again have to believe that circumstances outside of you control your life. . . . . We came here with a guaranteed freedom of choice mandated by the very nature of our existence. The time has come for us to exercise that birthright. We are caught in no one's web. We are bound by no circumstance. We are victims to no conditions. For we possess unregulated, unrestricted, uncontested freedom of choice, no matter what those choices may be. It's wake up time. It's time we remembered how to make those choices happen. (p. 25)

Here are the four steps to deliberate creation, the four steps that are guaranteed—that's right, guaranteed—to bring into your life whatever is your passion and much, much more . . . . Now they are yours, if you want them:

> *Step One: Identify what you DON'T want.*
> *Step Two: From that, identify what you DO want.*
> *Step Three: Get into the feeling place of what you want.*
> *Step Four: Expect, listen, and allow it to happen. (p.22)*

At the very least, I consider the author's viewpoint to offer some beliefs that are most empowering, especially for us as women. Too often, we have been tempted to play the victim, and complain about our lot. While it is true that we have plenty to complain about, it is also true that complaining is a dead end. How much better it is to focus our energies on what we want, individually and together, for our lives and our planet. When we want change for the better passionately, and can imagine it happen with strong, positive feelings, we are well on the way to creating it. I have tried out the author's principles and have found that they have worked in many wonderful ways in my life, often surprising me with their effectiveness. I invite you to explore, experiment, try what she suggests, and see what happens.

This question opens the door to experiencing our greatest power—that of being life-giving co-creators with The Creator, Who is Pure Loving Joyful Peaceful Energy, and more— the One in whose image we are created.

We have far more power, I believe, than we have realized or been able to use. To guide the use of that creative power, we need a clear, positive vision of what we want for ourselves. So—what do you want in your life? Focus on that. Imagine it. Feel it. And listen for guidance as to what your part is in making it happen.

In our N.E.W. circles, we did just that. We drew pictures or symbols of what we wanted and imagined for our own flourishing, and the flourishing of all. Interestingly, we discovered that what we wanted for ourselves as individuals and what we wanted for the world were at heart very similar. "It's all really one," remarked one of the women. "I want personal peace, and I want peace for the world. I want joy for me, and joy for everyone. Joyful people don't hurt others. I want health for me and health for the planet as well as all people. We are one!"

As we shared our pictures with each other, we could just feel the energy in the room and in each of us soar. It felt good! It gave us positive focus. It energized us. It empowered us. Each of us left the circle with a better sense of all the positive things that could happen in our lives as we opened the channels to Grace and Guidance through positive passion and imagination.

Question Seven:
What concrete actions could I/we take to manifest what I/we want?

I use the word "manifest" in this question deliberately, because it best expresses what I have been saying all along about taking action. What we believe shapes our actions, and belief involves both thought and feeling.

When a belief is a conviction, it much more powerfully shapes what we do than if what we want is just a wish. We must firmly believe that what we want is possible, desirable, and necessary. Then we must imagine what it would be like to have what we want, concretely and vividly. We must feel how good it would be, and then dwell on those wonderful feelings. Finally, we must open ourselves to Divine Wisdom and guidance about what action we can take to manifest what we want.

I found it interesting that when our N.E.W. circles talked about what we wanted, almost everything we came up with was very much like the visions for a better world held out in the sacred writings and traditions of the world's great religions and spiritualities. Native American Black Elk's mountain vision of the "sacred hoop" into which all the peoples of the world are gathered in peace and harmony is an example. The Bible's vision of a world in which there is no more hurting or destroying, and creation is renewed so that deserts blossom like gardens, and the lion lies down with the lamb is another. The Koran's vision of a just society is still another.

These best and greatest visions of the human heart are, I believe, the gift of the Great Mystery that created this universe. When our visions are in alignment with Divine Vision, there is all the more reason to believe that they can actually happen in this world. Amazing Grace breaks through and does the seemingly impossible in our world. Who thought the Communist empire could fall apart without terrible violence? Who thought apartheid in South Africa could fall without racial warfare? Who thought peaceful non-violent resistance could defeat the British Empire in India? Most people did not think so. But there were some great visionaries who did, and acted on their beliefs, and look at the results! They reveal the truth of the saying "God will not do for us what God cannot do through us."

However, it is sometimes hard for us to know what we really want. The greatest visions of humankind are a good place to start. Then we can work down to our individual lives and consult our inner Wisdom. Sometimes our childhood memories will also provide us with clues about what we really want. Joy is always a sure trail to follow. Whatever excites us, makes us feel joyful, or makes our hearts sing, is a sign of a desire that is good for us, because it expresses our true nature. It confirms whatever Divine guidance we have received. And what is truly good for us is good for everyone.

Remember, hope, faith, love, and joy are powerful feelings that attract the future we desire. We will receive Divine guidance as to what we need to do, personally and together. Moreover, Divine providence will provide what is needed to accomplish the tasks we are guided to undertake. These beliefs will, when accompanied by strong, positive feelings, and expressed in specific action, manifest what we want and what Godde wants.

In Chapter Two, I invited you to experience the real power of imagining a better and different future. Now, I invite you to do it again, alone, or with a friend or two or more. Really get into it! Be as concrete as you can. Feel those good feelings as strongly as you can. Listen for guidance. Then act.

Your life will never be the same. Your world will never be the same.

I am just one example that this is true. When I was inspired with the thought months ago, "Wouldn't it be wonderful if, everywhere in the world, there were circles to empower women, and any woman who wanted to could go to one when she needed and wanted empowerment?" I imagined that possibility for hours on end, and felt the excitement and joy of seeing it actually happen. I listened for guidance as to what to do, and got it. This book is one of the results. The already existing N.E.W. circles are another. The website which will be up and running when this book is published is still another. Already, women I know are planning on starting more circles this year.

I believe and imagine that this movement will grow, will catch fire, and that the Wind of the Spirit will blow it far and wide. All over this country, and all over the world, there will be N.E.W. circles. They will be part of a great, far-reaching, strong Network to Empower Women which, connected to other similar efforts already underway, will tip the balance in our favor as women. The Status Quo will fall apart, and the peaceful, flourishing world where men and women are full partners will happen. I believe I might even live to see it. And so might you! If you are reading this book, chances are good that you will be a part of this great movement, making it grow into its full potential and power.

So take the time to imagine, feel good, listen, and act. Who knows what wonderful things can happen for you and the world? Question Seven opens the door from a closed-in future determined by the past and the present Status Quo, to a wide-open future filled with possibilities very different from the way things are right now. It reminds us that it is up to us to believe, imagine, feel, and act concretely, and positively.

Question Eight:
How can I live with greater connection and support with women and girls in my circles, community, and the world?

The belief behind this question is that strong connection and support between women and girls is absolutely essential for the empowerment of women. Obviously, there is power in numbers. We are over half the population. We have enormous economic power. We are gaining every day in political power. We are certainly gaining spiritual power, within or outside of traditional religious institutions. In fact, within the institutions that oppress them, women are the majority!

Think of what would happen if we stopped attending and supporting with our time and money any religious organization that did not actively support the full equality of women. Where would schools, or businesses, or volunteer organizations, or the professions, or service industries like restaurants, hospitals, cleaning organizations, (and any others you can think of) be if we would withdraw our presence?

Perhaps we think first of how we might suffer by losing a job, losing status, losing approval. That is not an impossibility. Again, we need to ask ourselves what we are willing to suffer and risk for the greater good. Women like Susan B. Anthony and Rosa Parks in our country, and many other brave women in other countries, have set us an example in this regard. The kind of change we are after as women is not going to come cheaply and easily.

On the other hand, the truth is that most the structures of society, from home to business to government to education, to health care, etc. need us worse than we need them. This society could not function without our active co-operation. The status quo is built upon the back of women's unpaid labor in the home, and unequally paid labor in the rest of society.

As the Chinese say, "Women hold up half the sky." Think what that really means!

In order to keep us from realizing and acting on the real power we have, we are kept divided and isolated. Women and girls are encouraged to compete with each other for male attention. We are told we are not worth much if we can't attract and hold a man, and that we will never make it in life without one. Of course, there are women today who do not believe this, and their numbers are increasing. Unfortunately, they are still the minority of women. My husband once observed that the women who worked in many offices he knew of could not get along. I was not encouraged by his remark! It is all too true that we women are sometimes our own worst enemies. We can and do undermine, deceive, attack, and damage each other. This is exactly what the Domination System promotes, and to the degree it happens, we are prevented from the solidarity with each other that could empower us to break free into the full use of our innate power.

I believe that we women can get along very well indeed. I have often seen it happen. Even with our disagreements and differences, we know how to build relationships, if we want to. Yet, we still sometimes allow ourselves to unconsciously engage in behavior that prevents our potential unity as women, because that is what we have been programmed to do. Much of the conflict between us is because we feel individually so frustrated and powerless.

We also live all too often with less than we need: less help, less time, less support, less money, less sleep, etc. This condition of scarcity breeds competition, rather than co-operation. We must resist the urge to compete with each other and turn our energy instead to acting together so that through sharing our resources, our energy, and ideas, we can help change society so that all of us have enough of what we need.

When we overcome our negativity towards each other and realize that we have a much better chance of getting ahead if we make common cause with each other, real progress is possible. Women are not the enemy. The Status Quo is. United we stand, divided we fall. Our present challenge is to get together in circles in all institutions in society and find ways to help each other do well and make necessary changes wherever we live and work.

For instance, when I was the pastor of a large church, there was a seminary nearby where there were a few women students. They often attended the church, and they began to see the advantage of getting together, busy as they were, to encourage and support each other as a small minority in a male dominated institution. When they started to do this in the seminary cafeteria, they got all kinds of negative looks and remarks from the men, who were sure they were gathering to bash males, and who knows what else? The women students began to feel so uncomfortable, they came to me and asked if they could meet at the church instead, away from the hostile eyes of their fellow male students. Of course, I gladly agreed, and they enjoyed many wonderful meetings in a safe place, supporting each other in a difficult situation. Because they got together, they were able to initiate changes at the seminary that were long overdue.

We women really do need each other. We need each other to help raise our girls to be proud, strong, confident, powerful young women in a society that has thus far prevented many of them from becoming what they could be. We need to model what we want them to be. We need to celebrate the milestones in their lives and ours together, including the beginning and end of menstruation, the "changes of life" which are so ignored or scorned in our society. We also need to inoculate our girls and ourselves against the negative messages in the media. Think of how often we are portrayed as sex objects, as victims, or as of secondary importance.

The majority of movies still feature more men than women in the lead roles. The majority of the stories is about men's activities, and portrays men and women in the kind of roles that support the Status Quo. Ads for boys' toys feature war and action figures. Ads for girls' toys feature domestic and decorative activities and figures.

We need to spend our precious time and money in ways that support what supports us, and not anything else. Why watch television and commercials that are demeaning to us, when we could spend that time being together, in circles like those described in this book? Why spend time shopping when we don't need to, instead of spending that time with each other? Why not use lunch hours at work in a purposeful way to connect with other women to empower each other? Isn't it about time? An empowering women's circle could bring about many good changes in any school, religious organization, or business in which it formed. Women in Congress have discovered how useful it is to get together to help each other accomplish the goals they have chosen. Women all over the world are discovering the same thing. Some of what they are doing was described in Chapter One: The Power of Our Stories.

Thanks to the internet, telecommunications, and all the ways in which this world is now connected as never before, we have the opportunity to also connect with women and girls in other countries. Organizations like ChildReach emphasize empowering women and girls, and I have chosen to sponsor a girl in India through them. My daughter has had two little sisters through the Big Sister Program, which is also a good channel for connection between women and girls. Others are listed in the Resource Appendix.

For too long, we have been divided and therefore conquered by the Domination System of the Status Quo. We can make sure that time is now over. Questions Eight opens the door out of isolation and fear into a scene of celebration as millions of women discover how powerful they are, together.

The Re-Imagining conference that took place a few years ago in Minneapolis is a prime example of this. Over five thousand women from various religious organizations, ethnic groups, and parts of society gathered to re-imagine the world as women would like to see it. I wish you could have been there. The energy was enormous! One man sitting next to me (there were a few good men there!) whispered in my ear, "I have never seen this kind of energy generated by meetings led by men!" Those thousands of women sang and laughed and cried and danced and listened and left permanently changed as they experienced the power of women gathered for the purpose of re-imagining and accordingly changing things. It was so threatening to the Status Quo that many churches punished the women who had been a part of this historic conference. The movement still goes on, and many more like it, not only in this country, but also all over the world.

Nothing can stop us now!

Nothing, that is, if we connect with other women and girls deliberately, intentionally, as a top priority in our lives. We have great power when we consciously work to empower each other, and work together on creating the life-giving changes we want. One woman in our N.E.W. circles who is a great example of someone who is doing this recently said at one of our meetings, "I am too busy not to come!"

Question Nine:
Your choice!

You get to choose this question, because it is so important for you to experience, in this way, the power of choosing for yourself. You have read the Eight Questions that are at the heart of the N.E.W. circle process.

If you have not personally explored them yet, I encourage you to do so, perhaps by taking a little time each day or week to ponder each one, and write down what comes to you. If it helps to do it with a friend, by all means do so. Of course, being a part of a N.E.W. circle is ideal. All you need are two or more friends, and this guidebook. Working with the previous eight questions will prepare you for finding just the right ninth question for you. It is important for each person in a N.E.W. circle to spend some quality time pondering what her choice for question nine will be.

Here are a few of the questions we came up with in our N.E.W. circles when we considered what the Ninth question might be for us.

1. How can I pass on what I am experiencing in this N.E.W. circle to my daughters and granddaughters so they can be empowered early on in their lives?

2. What kind of rituals would be most empowering for us as girls and women in our culture to celebrate the milestones in our lives?
3. How can we draw women of various ethnic and cultural and economic backgrounds together into circles, so they are truly diverse, and create strong bonds across social divisions?
4. How can I switch from judgment to discernment, so that I live more compassionately and wisely?

Here are a few quotes to inspire you as you consider what you might choose as a question that would most help you continue in an empowering process.

"The important thing is, not to stop questioning." (Albert Einstein)

"We shall not cease from our exploring, and the end of our exploring will be to return to the place we started and know it for the first time." —T.S. Eliot

. . . . I would like to beg you . . . to have patience with everything unresolved in your heart, and to try to love the questions themselves as if they were locked rooms or books written in a foreign language . . . . And the point is, to live everything. Live the questions now. Perhaps then, someday far in the future, you will gradually, without even noticing it, live your way into the answer." —Rainer Maria Rilke

Now it is up to you to choose the Ninth Question.

I would love to know what questions you came up with. You can email me at *Marchiene@earthlink.net,* or go to our website, *www.networktoempowerwomen.com.*

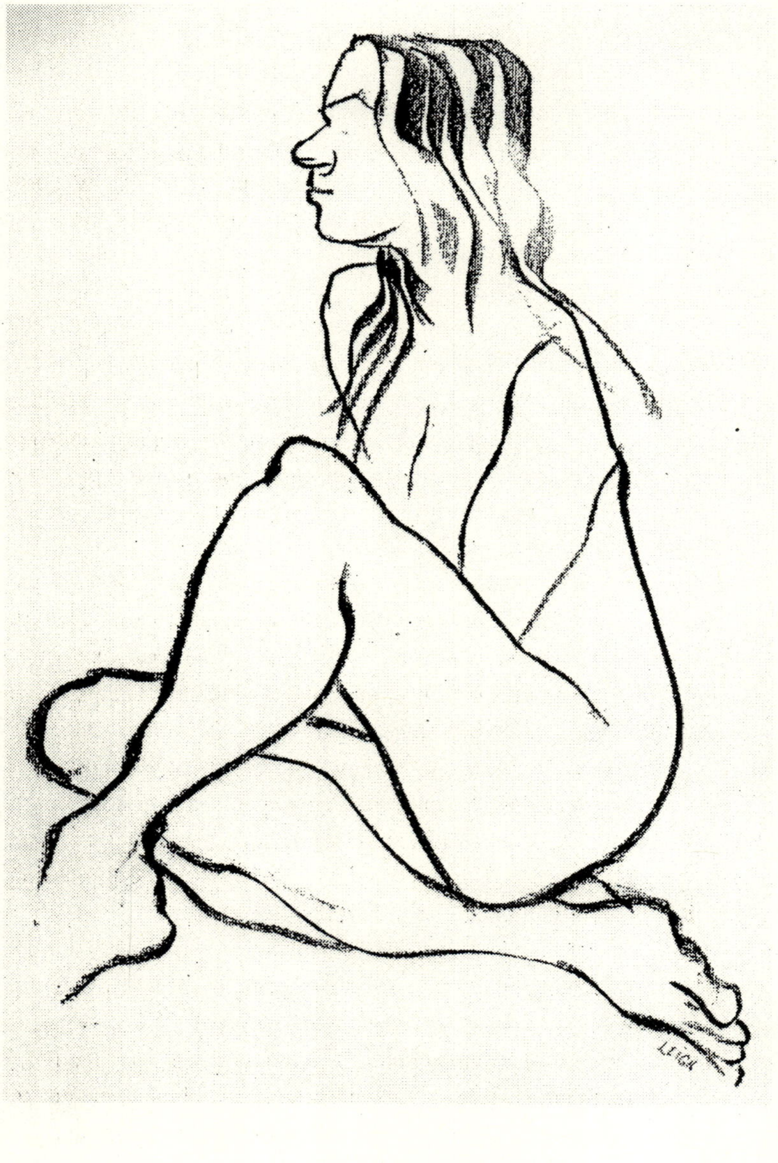
LEIGH

CHAPTER FIVE

THE POWER OF EXPERIENCE

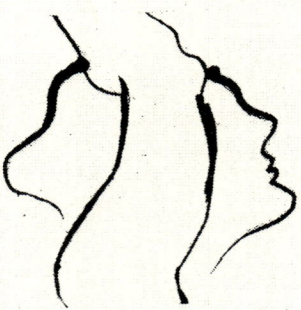

"Experience" as they say, "is the best teacher." Something can look and sound good on paper, or in spoken words, but until it actually turns into experience, it is not "tried and true." You don't really know what works and what doesn't. This chapter introduces you, the reader, to N.E.W. circles in action. You have already been reading about the vision and goals for the Network to Empower Women, the process and agreements the N.E.W. circles use, and the Nine Questions that are considered, turn by turn, at each meeting. Now I want to tell you how an actual meeting goes, based on experience.

I will describe a particular meeting—the first one, and then one other, so that you can get a good feel for what a N.E.W. circle is like. Of course, if you choose to start one, or join one, and I hope you do, you will find that every circle has its own unique character, depending on who comes, where it meets, how long the circle meets, how many women are there, and more.

That said, I can say from experience that what makes a women's circle a N.E.W. circle—that is, the format, the process, and the questions—works well. The women who have come more than once have found it a powerful, significant experience in their lives. The way the circle is conducted provides a safe, dependable structure that honors each woman. The questions quickly take participants to an important place within themselves, and begin a process that continues long after the circle meeting is over. There is a marvelous, sometimes surprising openheartedness, vulnerability, and depth of sharing which every woman treasures. The things we have learned from each other have been inspiring and life changing. The support we feel in the circle from one another has helped us all immeasurably.

Come, and join me with your imagination as a N.E.W. circle gathers for the first time.

It is early Sunday morning—8:30 a.m. to be exact. This is the best time for the women who have agreed to be a part of one of the first N.E.W. circles. Most of us have obligations on Sunday the whole rest of the day. Yet we are willing to get up early and come together, eager to find out what N.E.W. is all about and what kind of experience it will be for us.

The place we are meeting is a small massage therapist's office behind a coffee shop. The owner of the space is also one of the women interested in this venture. She is offering it to the rest of us free of charge. But we have a basket handy into which women can put a small donation to help pay for the cost of opening and warming and lighting her cozy space on a cold morning.

When we enter the room, we find a circle of chairs already set up for us, with a small table in the center. On it are a candle, a small bowl of stones, a beautiful round glass ball on a little stand, and a bell. As we each find a seat, we look at each other, noticing that there are both familiar and unfamiliar faces. Once we are settled, I introduce myself, tell a little of how the idea of N.E.W. circles came to be, and what they can expect. I hand out a guide to the N.E.W. process for this first meeting to each person. (The guides we use for each meeting can be found in this chapter after the description of the two circle meetings.)

We each introduce ourselves briefly, simply stating our first name and why we have come. "I just want to see what this is about," says one. "I want to be supportive because I believe in empowering women," says another. "I need other women to help me deal with my life," adds a third. There is an exciting sense of anticipation in the air as we go around the circle. When all seven women have had their turns, I thank them for being willing to go on this adventure as one of the pioneer circles of the Network to Empower Women. I invite them to offer their feedback as we go through the guide sheets for the first time, and also to offer their feedback after the meeting or by email. We send around a sheet of paper on which each woman who wishes to may write her name and address, phone number, or/ and e-mail.

Now we are ready to enter into sacred time and space.

Someone lights the candle, and strikes the bell gently.

A hush falls over the room as everyone falls silent.

"Take three deep breaths, in through your nose and out through your mouth," I say. "Relax. Be comfortable, with both feet on the floor. Now imagine the candle light filling each person in this room with its bright, glowing radiance." I pause for a few moments, and then continue. "Now imagine the whole room filling with this light, and feel the peace and joy that it contains." We sit in silence for a few more moments. "Now, when you are ready, open your eyes," I say. Soon, everyone's eyes are open. Each face looks calmer, each woman more relaxed. We are ready.

"As always," I begin, "we read the purpose and vision of N.E.W. first. This is to remind us what we are here for, and for the benefit of any newcomers at future meetings. Then we read the Nine Agreements for how a N.E.W. circle functions, and the Nine Questions we explore at our meetings. This is so that everyone is clear about what to expect and how our process works. It is designed to provide a safe, strong structure within which we can openly explore and share." The women nod, and some look especially relieved. They have probably been at too many meetings in which there were no clear guidelines, and all sorts of problems arose as a result.

Taking turns, we each read the material I have handed out. I make it clear that no one must read aloud, and they can simply pass if they don't want to. Everyone takes a turn reading, and at the end, I invite any comments or questions. This is because it is the first meeting. Normally, I would not do this. I explain this, and add that, as the leader this time, I want to honor our agreed upon one and a half hour time limit. I know some of them will need to leave right on time. A few women offer suggestions, and then we are ready for the heart of the meeting: the time of sharing.

I slowly take the glass ball off the table at the center and hold it in my hand. The blue and green pattern within it looks like the world enclosed in glass. "I chose this as our talking object today, because it reminds me that the world is waiting for us women to step forward and take our turn. Men need us as partners with them to help create a flourishing future for everyone and for the planet itself. What we are starting here this morning is a step in that direction. And you are a part of it." I hold out the ball so everyone can see it, and notice the smiles all around the room.

"Today," I continue, "I invite each of you, by turn, to hold this ball in your hand, and while holding it, tell us what you are grateful to have survived and accomplished, and who or what has empowered you in your life thus far. You can respond to all or any part of this question. As you speak, we will all listen with open hearts and loving attention, silently.

We will let our silence support you as you speak. When you are done, you can pass the ball to the woman on your left. Then she will do the same, and so on around the room. If any one of you does not wish to speak when the ball is passed to you, you can simply pass it on to the next woman in silence. After everyone has had a chance, there will be an opportunity for any woman who has something to say to share it at that point in the same way we are sharing now."

I begin, feeling that as the leader, I need to model what I am talking about. As I hold the ball, I talk about what I have survived: serious childhood illness, breast cancer, and serious opposition to women in ministry. I talk of my accomplishments. I notice I feel a little reluctance to do so. I have been brought up to never "toot your own horn." But I persist through my reluctance as I speak of having raised four children who have become wonderful young men and women, of having been the first woman minister in the denomination I grew up in, of having learned how to paint, and of having published three books and many articles. I describe my two grandmothers, and the strong single women I grew up with during my childhood in India, as women who empowered me by their example and loving attention.

It feels so good to be heard without interruption, the other women's faces mirroring their feelings as I speak. I know my words have already sparked lots of thoughts and feelings in them. When I am done, I pass the ball to the woman on my left, and she begins. She tells of a father who strongly encouraged her to be all she could be, and helped her face many challenges. She speaks of the challenges she overcame as the only girl in a large family of boys. She speaks of her achievement in making a good home for her two girls after a painful divorce. We all listen with rapt attention. The room is quiet, full of loving energy. When she is done, there are tears in some eyes.

The ball goes to the next woman, and once again we listen supportively as she speaks. Our body language and faces say "We are with you. We hear you. We want to understand what it is like for you." By the time the ball has gone around the room, and every woman has spoken, there is a strong sense of bonding between us. Some of us have just met, yet we feel that we know each other already in a deeper way than we know some people we have met many times.

Now each woman in turn goes to the Center of the circle, and taking a stone from the bowl there, places it on the table as she names and honors people who have empowered her. When we are done with this simple ritual, we have created a small altar of stones, a visible reminder of what we have shared and those we have honored with hearts full of gratitude.

Finally, we stand in a circle, and sing the second verse of "Amazing Grace." *Through many dangers, toils, and snares, we have already come. 'Tis Grace that brought us safe thus far, and Grace will lead us Home.* The blending of our voices in a familiar song seems just right as a closing ritual for our meeting.

The meeting is over. We break the circle, and someone says, "I think Amazing Grace is a great name for God." We all laugh, and then I say, "Wait! Leadership is shared in this circle, remember? Is anyone willing to lead the next meeting? You know how they go now. As the leader, you can choose the opening and closing ritual and take us through the process the way I did. It's all on the circle meeting guide sheet. Anyone can do it!"

After a moment's hesitation, one of the women volunteers. "It seems pretty simple," she says. "And I know I'll have help."

"Thank you!" I exclaim. "I think we have made a wonderful beginning."

*   *   *

Now it is a couple of months later. It is Saturday morning at 10 a.m. and another N.E.W. circle is meeting, this time in a counseling center office. It belongs to one of the women who is attending the circle meetings regularly.

She has set up a circle of chairs for us, and on a small table in the center is a large blue and purple candle, some incense, a bell, a beautiful Native American talking stick, and small vigil light candles arranged in a circle around them. A little box of matches is tucked under the table. As women come into this inviting space, they greet each other warmly. They are beginning to feel like old friends. There are also a couple of new women, and everyone makes a special effort to make them feel at home. They seem to appreciate the printed guideline for the meeting that is handed out to everyone as we sit down. I can see them scanning it as we get started.

Once again, we go around the circle, with each woman telling her name and why she has come. "I'm here because I really want to be. It's worth getting up on a Saturday morning to do this. I always feel so much better after being here," says one. "A friend told me about it and invited me to try it, so here I am," says another. "I saw a sign up in the coffee shop about it and thought I'd see what was going on," adds a young woman who looks a bit uncomfortable, as if she has stumbled into something she may regret. "I remember feeling a little uneasy the first time I came to a N.E.W. circle," says a woman next to her with a smile. "But it was a good experience for me, and feels not only comfortable, but very supportive now."

The woman in whose office we are meeting is the leader today. When everyone has introduced herself, she lights the candle, and then the incense. "If anyone is bothered by incense, let me know, and I can put it out," she says before she lights it. No one objects, so she goes ahead, remarking that for her, fragrance is a good way to create sacred space and time. As the smoke from the incense curls upward into the candlelight, the leader asks us to close our eyes as she leads in a brief meditation. She invites us to imagine we are walking over a bridge and down a path to a beautiful garden. There, we meet someone who offers us a special blessing. Each one is encouraged to imagine who that person is and how she receives the blessing in her own way. Then the leader tells us to walk back over the bridge and into the present, and when we are ready, open our eyes. There is a sense of peace in the room, and I can tell by some women's faces that this brief imaginary experience was very powerful for them.

When everyone is ready, the leader rings the bell, and invites us to join her in reading the purpose and vision for N.E.W., the Nine Agreements, and the Nine Questions. One of the regular members offers to meet with the newcomers after the meeting to answer any questions they may have about the circle and how it operates.

Then the leader goes to the center and picks up the talking stick. "Today, we are going to explore Question Three," she says. "How have I found and followed my Inner Authority? How will I continue to do so?" As each of you holds this special talking stick, we will listen silently, with open hearts, as you speak. When you are finished, before you pass the talking stick on to the next woman, please go to the Center and light one of the vigil lights from the center candle as a symbol of the light of your own Inner Wisdom. We all light our candles from the flame of the One Holy Wisdom that shines in our hearts." With this simple explanation, the sharing begins.

"This is a hard question for me," says the first woman to hold the talking stick. "I really never thought that I had Inner Authority. I have always looked for it outside of myself." She looks around the room at the other faces. "I don't know about you, but I think that's been one of my problems. I listen to this person and that person, this authority and that authority, and I get all confused. Which one is right? How do I know? And how do I find my own Inner Authority so I can sort it all out? I don't have an answer to that yet. I hope some of you do. That's all." She looks at the leader. "Can I still light a candle?" she asks, with a little tremor in her voice. The leader nods and smiles her encouragement. The young woman slowly walks to the Center. The candlelight shines on her face as she bends down over the flame, and lights her own little candle from it. Reverently, she places it on the table and gazes at its flickering light for a long moment. Then, with a satisfied sigh, she sits down, and hands the talking stick to the woman on her left.

"I feel my Inner Authority when I meditate and when I am with other women like this," she says. "My alone time connects me to my soul, and that's where I feel my Inner Authority is. Sometimes I read an inspiring book as I drink a cup of coffee, sometimes I just stare out the window at a beautiful tree that grows in my yard, and sometimes I write in my journal. When I am with women who have a sense of connection to their own Inner Authority, I can feel it, and it empowers me." She gets up, lights a candle, and passes the talking stick on to the next woman.

"I get connected with my Inner Authority when I withdraw now and then from the mainstream of society, and go on retreat," she says. "And when I question things—that helps too. I don't just accept things the way they are. And I don't accept other people's answers unless they feel right to me. I'm going to keep going on retreat so I don't lose touch with my Inner Authority, and I think I'll try taking time in the morning or at night to meditate in some way every day too." She glances at the woman next to her who talked about her daily alone time, then lights her candle, and passes the talking stick on to the next woman.

"Believe it or not," she begins, "I first got in touch with my Inner Authority as a single mother with children. I had to be sure about some things, because I was responsible for their welfare. I realized I had some wisdom inside me, and as I discovered and shared it, I trusted myself more. As a mother, I was the number one authority in my children's lives, and I felt a sense of authority from the way they looked to me for guidance and answers. Now that they are teenagers, they are testing my confidence in my inner wisdom, but I think I'll make it! And oh yes, I've discovered that working with my dreams is really helping me experience the Wisdom deep within me." She smiles and lights a candle, and passes the stick on to the next woman.

When all of us have had a chance to speak, and the last woman lights her candle, a hush falls over the room. Everyone gazes at the circle of candles glowing around the large central candle. "We are all seeing our own Inner Authority made visible," I think as I look around the room. "This is a sacred moment!"

The leader invites us all to stand. "Everyone take your candle and hold it up high," she says. When we have done so, she laughs and says, "I bet a lot of you remember the children's song, *This little light of mine, I'm gonna let it shine*. Let's sing it together, and if anyone doesn't know it, they'll learn it quickly, it's so simple. And let's sing the second verse too—*Hide it under a bushel, NO, I'm gonna let it shine."* Everyone nods, and as we hold up our candles, we sing the familiar song with big smiles on our faces. When we are done, we put the candles back on the table, and the leader blows them all out, signifying the end of the meeting.

"Before you go—who will volunteer to lead the next one?" she asks. Someone volunteers, and the meeting breaks up into twos and threes as the women talk with each other, and exchange phone numbers and email addresses so they can be in contact in between meetings.

*   *   *

Now that you have attended two N.E.W. circle meetings by reading the two descriptions of them, I invite you to consider how you might start one of your own. All it takes is you, a couple of friends (or more) and a safe, accessible place in your community. To help you in your efforts, you will find below the meeting guidelines we have used for each of our meetings. There is one for every Question. I recommend you take a month for each question, meeting once, twice, or more a month to explore it.

First, however, I want to say a couple of things about the ways N.E.W. circles can function in very different cultures and circumstances. My experience with N.E.W. circles so far has been in the United States with mostly middle-class, Anglo women. My dream is that N.E.W. circles will quickly become multi-ethnic, multi-cultural, and global!

My approach is geared for the context in which it was created. But I have spent years in Africa and India, living among poor people. I am well aware of the fact that many people can't read, and don't have access to some of the materials described above. It is my experience that women can meet in any circumstances: under a tree outside, in a simple one room mud home, in a local school building, or wherever the possibilities open up. Women can and do gather in a circle sitting on the earth. I can imagine them creating the Center with a simple cloth, a circle of stones, or a design drawn in the dirt. The rituals described in the material in this book can be modified to suit the resources and context in which the women who meet find themselves. Women who cannot read, being blessed with better memories than literate people, can easily memorize the Goal, Vision, Agreements, and Questions. These too, can be simplified and modified to suit the women who use them. I have no desire to control how this material is used. The important thing is that it works for those who use it. Women are perfectly capable of figuring out creative ways of adapting it in the best ways!

I would love to hear of these ways from women who do so. I am glad that all over the world today, one can find Internet cafes and people to help one use them—even in small villages in underdeveloped areas. We can weave a world wide web of empowered women with these tools, if we want to. With the help of women from many social strata, cultures, and ethnic backgrounds, N.E.W. circles can flourish in many kinds of situations around the world. This is my hope and my dream. I am open to and grateful for any and all suggestions that will help this dream come true. By the time this book is published, the website for N.E.W. *www.networktoempowerwomen.com*. will be in place. There will be a special space on the web site for contributions from women who wish to help N.E.W. become all it can be. Meanwhile, I am also open to suggestions via email at *Marchiene@earthlink.net*. I'll be waiting! And I will incorporate all helpful suggestions in the forthcoming editions of this book.

Here, then, are the meeting guidelines we have been using:

A note to the leaders of the circles:

You will notice that the suggested rituals involve a few simple objects that need to be assembled ahead of time and taken to the meeting if you are the leader. You can, of course, always ask other women to help you get some of these things. A list of what you will need if you follow the suggested rituals is found before each meeting guide begins.

You will also notice, if you follow the suggested rituals, that many times the closing ritual invites the women who attended to take a little something home with them which reminds them of the circle and the process they are in. Please encourage those who attend the circle meetings to have a special space in their house to keep these material reminders as a way of remembering their connection to the circle and its process in between meetings.

The first N.E.W. Circle meeting guide is given below so that you have a clear idea of just how a meeting goes. Following the first meeting guide, the particular materials and ritual for each of the meetings for the Nine Questions is described. The material that is repeated at every meeting, i.e. the Purpose and Vision of N.E.W., the Nine Agreements, and the Nine Questions, are not repeated for every meeting here.

If you desire to use complete printed guides for the rest of the meetings, you will find them at the back of the book for you to copy and use as you wish.

CIRCLE MEETING GUIDE: FIRST QUESTION MEETING

Note: The leader of this meeting who chooses to use the suggested rituals will need to bring a candle, matches, a bell, a talking object, (ball, stone, stick, feather, flower, etc.) and a bowl of stones.

Welcome: Each woman says her name and why she has come.

Opening Ritual: The leader lights a candle or rings a bell, and leads the group in an opening moment of silence and centering.

Suggestion: Ask participants to take three deep breaths; close their eyes, and imagine Light filling each person, and the whole room. After a few moments of silence, invite them to open their eyes.

THE FUTURE FOR WOMEN - A N.E.W. BOOK

READING OF THE PURPOSE AND VISION, NINE AGREEMENTS, AND NINE QUESTIONS:

The leader hands out a printed copy of the Purpose and Vision for N.E.W., the Nine Agreements for circle process, and the Nine Questions. The leader and participants take turns reading them out loud. Questions and comments about these are welcome after the meeting is over. Alternatively, the leader or someone else present can simply read the material below out loud so everyone can hear.

THE PURPOSE AND VISION FOR N.E.W.

The purpose of the Network to Empower Women is to create and develop a circle-process and link women and resources on the World Wide Web in a way that enables the empowering of women everywhere.

Power is understood as the ability to help people and all of life flourish.

It has nothing to do with domination or control.

It does have to do with the ability to create, choose, and act for the flourishing of oneself and all creation.

Women need to be able to use their innate power for this purpose, so that humanity can finally become like a bird that is flying, because it is using both wings.

Women and men need to fly together in every arena of society.

Women's gifts and wisdom are desperately needed if the world is to have a flourishing future.

The vision for N.E. W. is a worldwide network of circles that intentionally empower women, meeting in as many places as possible, linked with the many other resources and organizations already empowering women.

THE NINE AGREEMENTS FOR NEW CIRCLES

1. We meet in a circle with a Center that symbolizes the Wisdom within and among us.

2. We all listen as each one speaks in turn, using a symbolic object. We do not interrupt, cross talk, or give advice during the meeting.
3. We honor and respect the confidentiality of what is spoken in the circle.
4. We honor each one's contribution, listen without judgment, and support each other in a loving manner.
5. We all take responsibility for the process of the group, honoring time constraints and the agreements that guide the circle. Leadership is shared and rotated.
6. We exercise our personal right to refrain from any activity that violates our boundaries.
7. We all rely on the Wisdom of the circle's center and in each of us. The circle is like a wheel with each person connected to the hub at the center. To remain centered, we observe a brief silence between each woman's reflections, and at any time during the meeting someone asks for it.
8. In between meetings, we connect with each other in order to help one another continue to explore the questions of the N.E.W. process, and offer support as needed. We especially reach out to those who are new to the circle meetings and process.
9. We want to reach out to as many women as possible in order to accomplish the vision of N.E.W. Therefore, we meet in a public location, safe, free of interruption, and open to any woman who wishes to attend.

We may collect a small fee at the meeting to defray any expenses. The time frame can be as short as an hour once a week, or a couple of hours once or twice a month.

We cover one of the Questions at each meeting, and repeat the cycle of Nine Questions as often as desired.

Ideally, there are NEW circles meeting in many places at many times so that a woman can always find one when she wants it.

THE NINE QUESTION PROCESS (PARTICIPANTS MAY CHOOSE ONE OR MORE PARTS OF A QUESTION THAT HAS MULTIPLE PARTS.)

1. What am I grateful to have survived? Accomplished? Who or what has empowered me in my life so far?

2. What damaging, false beliefs about myself and/or women do I want to release? What healing, helpful beliefs do I want to affirm and live?
3. How have I found and followed my own Inner Authority? How will I continue to do so?
4. What are the spiritual practices and resources that empower me?
5. What obstacles to using my innate power as a woman have I/we encountered? What are some strategies for dealing with them? How do I stop giving away my power?
6. What can I imagine, and what do I want for my flourishing and the flourishing of all?
7. What concrete actions could I/we take to manifest what I/we want?
8. How can I live with greater connection and support with women and girls in my circles, community, and the world?
9. Free choice

EXPLORING QUESTION ONE:

What am I grateful to have survived? Accomplished?
Who or what has empowered me in my life so far?
  A talking object, such as a stone, stick, feather, etc. is passed from woman to woman as each one speaks. While holding the object, each woman has an opportunity to reflect upon Question One. When she is done, she puts a stone in the center of the circle honoring someone who has empowered her.
  After all have shared, an opportunity is given, if there is time, for those who have not spoken or wish to say something more to do so.

The meeting closes with a ritual of some kind: a song, a prayer, a moment of silence, etc.

Suggestion: The leader invites the women to stand together in a circle. She takes a stone and passes it around the circle, asking each woman to hold it in her hand and put the warmth of blessing energy into it. Then she passes the stone to the next woman, who receives its blessing energy

as she holds it, adds her own to it, and passes it on, until it has gone around the circle.

The leader recites a blessing she chooses for the occasion. Each woman is then invited to take a stone from the table at the Center home with her and put it in a place that will remind her of the blessing and support of the circle.

Someone volunteers to lead the next circle meeting. All are encouraged to take a few moments before leaving to pair up and arrange for a way to connect with each other between meetings.

CIRCLE MEETING GUIDE FOR SECOND QUESTION MEETING

Note: The leader of the second meeting (see below) who chooses to use the suggested rituals will need to bring a candle, matches, a bell, a talking object, (ball, stone, stick, feather, flower, etc.) a fireproof container in which to burn paper, thin, easily burnable paper on which to write, and pencils or pens, a vase, and flowers for everyone. (Always have more than enough!)

Welcome: Each woman says her name and why she has come, or (briefly!) anything else she chooses.

Opening Ritual: The leader lights a candle, rings a bell, or drums, or plays a musical instrument to call the group together, and leads the group in an opening moment of silence and centering or a brief meditation suited to the question of the day.

Suggestion: Everyone stands and takes three deep breaths, in through the nose, and out through the mouth, with eyes closed. Then everyone imagines that there are silver roots growing from the soles of their feet deep down into Mother Earth—300 feet or more.

After a few moments of silence, all are seated.

EXPLORING QUESTION TWO:

What damaging, false beliefs about myself and/or women do I want to release?
What healing, helpful beliefs do I want to affirm and live?

Everyone is given a piece of paper that burns quickly and easily, and something to write with. After everyone has held the talking object and had a chance to reflect on the first half of this question, the talking object is placed in the Center while participants write down symbols or words of beliefs they would like to release. When all are ready, one at a time, each puts her paper in a fireproof container in the center, and lights a match to it.

When it has burned up, it is the next woman's turn. There is silence during this time.

Next, the talking object is passed around again, and each woman has a chance to reflect on the second part of the question. This time, when she is done, she takes a flower from a pile of flowers on the floor near the center, and places it in a vase that is in the Center.

When everyone has had a turn, there is a bouquet of flowers, and a container of ashes in the Center, symbolizing beliefs that have been released and beliefs that have been affirmed by each woman.

The meeting closes with a ritual of some kind: a song, a prayer, a moment of silence, etc.

Suggestion: The leader asks the women to stand together in a circle. She passes the vase of flowers around. Each woman takes her flower back out of the vase as it is passed around the circle so she can take it home and put it in a place that reminds her of the beliefs she and others in the circle have chosen to affirm and live. A song, prayer, quote, or blessing may be offered.

Someone volunteers to lead the next circle meeting. All are encouraged to take a few moments before leaving to pair up and arrange for a way to connect with each other between meetings.

CIRCLE MEETING GUIDE: THIRD QUESTION MEETING

Note: The leader of the third meeting (see below) who chooses to use the suggested rituals will need to bring a candle, matches, a bell, drum, or musical instrument, a talking object, (ball, stone, stick, feather, flower, etc) and enough small vigil lights or candles for all the participants.

Welcome: Each woman says her name and why she has come, or (briefly!) anything else she chooses.

Opening Ritual: The leader lights a candle, rings a bell, or drums, or plays a musical instrument to call the group together, and leads the group in an opening moment of silence and centering or a brief meditation suited to the question of the day.

Suggestion: Ask participants to take three deep breaths, close their eyes, and imagine Light filling each person, and the whole room. After a few moments of silence, invite them to open their eyes.

READING OF THE PURPOSE AND VISION, NINE AGREEMENTS, AND NINE QUESTIONS:

EXPLORING QUESTION THREE:

How have I found and followed my own Inner Authority?
How will I continue to do so?

In the Center there is a ring of small candles, or vigil lights, arranged around a larger central candle. The leader starts the talking object going around the circle. After each woman holds the object and responds to Question Three, she lights one of the little candles from the big candle as a symbol of her inner authority and its connection to the Wisdom that shines in every woman. When everyone has had a chance to respond to the question and light a candle, the circle sits in silence, absorbing the lights they have lit and what they mean.

The meeting closes with a ritual of some kind: a song, a prayer, a moment of silence, etc.

Suggestion: The leader asks the women to stand together in a circle. She asks them to hold their candles high above their heads while singing "This little light of mine, I'm gonna let it shine" or some other appropriate song. Or, a quote or prayer may be offered that reflects the light of women's authority and wisdom.

Someone volunteers to lead the next circle meeting. (Note: not every woman has to take a turn leading, but it is important that leadership is rotated and shared by at least some of the women, so that the circle does not become dominated by one leader.) All are encouraged to take a few moments before leaving to pair up and arrange for a way to connect with each other between meetings.

CIRCLE MEETING GUIDE: FOURTH QUESTION MEETING

Note: The leader of the fourth meeting (see below) who chooses to use the suggested rituals will need to bring a candle, matches, a bell, drum, or musical instrument, a talking object, (ball, stone, stick, feather, flower, etc) a little bowl of seeds (sunflower seeds work well, but use whatever is available) and a container with soil in it for each participant. Mugs, small clay pots, little baskets with lining to keep the moisture in—all work well. (Check the local flea market or ask around for cups no one wants to save expense)

Welcome: Each woman says her name and why she has come, or (briefly!) anything else she chooses.

Opening Ritual: The leader lights a candle, rings a bell, or drums, or plays a musical instrument to call the group together, and leads the group in an opening moment of silence and centering or a brief meditation suited to the question of the day.

Suggestion: Everyone stands and takes three deep breaths, in through the nose, and out through the mouth, with eyes closed. Then everyone imagines that there are silver roots growing from the soles of their feet deep down into Mother Earth—300 feet or more.

After a few moments of silence, all are seated.

READING OF THE PURPOSE AND VISION, NINE AGREEMENTS, AND NINE QUESTIONS:

EXPLORING QUESTION FOUR:

What are the spiritual practices and resources that empower me?

The leader passes a talking object around the circle, inviting each woman to respond to this question as she holds it, and the others silently listen. There is one container for each person, filled with soil, and a pile of seeds in the Center. After each woman speaks, she plants sunflower (or other type) seeds in a little container that has soil in it, leaving it in the Center.

When everyone has had a chance to speak, each of the women takes her container of seeds as a sign of her commitment to use the spiritual practices and resources that empower her. The leader encourages each woman to take the container home and keep it in a place where she will water it, watch it grow, and let it remind her to let her commitment grow and blossom.

The meeting closes with a song, a prayer, a moment of silence, etc.

Someone volunteers to lead the next circle meeting. (Note: Not every woman has to take a turn leading, but it is important that leadership is rotated and shared by at least some of the women, so that the circle does not become dominated by one leader.) All are encouraged to take a few moments before leaving to pair up and arrange for a way to connect with each other between meetings.

CIRCLE MEETING GUIDE: FIFTH QUESTION MEETING

Note: The leader of the fifth meeting (see below) who chooses to use the suggested rituals will need to bring a candle, matches, a bell, drum, or musical instrument, a talking object, which in this case is a small bowl or glass or chalice of perfumed oil which will also be used for the ritual association with Question Five.

Welcome: Each woman says her name and why she has come, or (briefly!) anything else she chooses.

Opening Ritual: The leader lights a candle, rings a bell, or drums, or plays a musical instrument to call the group together, and leads the group in an opening moment of silence and centering or a brief meditation suited to the question of the day.

Suggestion: The leader asks everyone to take a couple deep breaths, close their eyes, and relax. Then she says, "Imagine you are in a race. You are at the starting line, looking down the racetrack ahead of you, anticipating the run. As you leave the starting line and round the first turn of the track, you notice a series of hurdles in front of you. You were not expecting them, but you realize you have to jump over them to continue the race. You keep running towards them while in your mind's eye you see yourself leaping easily over each of them. And you do! You can feel the wind in your hair as your legs clear the hurdles with room to spare, and you continue on your race. You run with great exhilaration, because you were able to take the hurdles in stride. Feel the exhilaration. Stay with the feeling . . . . Now, gradually come back to the present, take a couple deep breaths, and open your eyes."

When all are ready, the leader begins the rest of the meeting.

READING OF THE PURPOSE AND VISION, NINE AGREEMENTS, AND NINE QUESTIONS:

EXPLORING QUESTION FIVE:

What obstacles to using my innate power as a woman have I/we encountered?
What are some strategies for dealing with them?
How do I stop giving away my power?

There is a small bowl, cup, or chalice of perfumed oil in the Center of the circle. The leader takes the container as the talking object for the

exploring of Question Five. As each woman speaks, she holds the container of oil in her hands. When she is done, the other women in the circle come up to her, one by one, and in silence anoint her with a spiral on the forehead, throat, hands, top of head, or wherever the woman holding the oil prefers. She receives this anointing as an empowering blessing, and a sign of Divine Authority to do what she had been gifted and led to do and be. The anointed woman then passes the bowl to the woman next to her, and the process is repeated.

When everyone has had a chance to speak, and has been anointed, all the women stand and together dip their finger in the container of oil in the Center of the circle, turn outward facing the world, and make a spiral in the air with their oiled finger. This is a sign of blessing the world with women's power, and of moving freely through any obstacles around the spiral of their power.

Finally, all face each other in a circle again, and holding hands sing "We shall Overcome" or another suitable song or chant. The leader may substitute or add a quote, or prayer or affirmations for overcoming obstacles.

Someone volunteers to lead the next circle meeting. (Note: Not every woman has to take a turn leading, but it is important that leadership is rotated and shared by at least some of the women, so that the circle does not become dominated by one leader.) All are encouraged to take a few moments before leaving to pair up and arrange for a way to connect with each other between meetings.

CIRCLE MEETING GUIDE: SIXTH QUESTION MEETING

Note: The leader of the sixth meeting (see below) who chooses to use the suggested rituals will need to bring a candle, matches, a bell, drum, or musical instrument, a talking object, which in this case is a ball of clay about the size of a peach or large lemon, plain paper and crayons, markers, pastels or whatever is available for drawing.

Welcome: Each woman says her name and why she has come, or (briefly!) anything else she chooses.

Opening Ritual: The leader lights a candle, rings a bell, or drums, or plays a musical instrument to call the group together, and leads the group in an opening moment of silence and centering or a brief meditation suited to the question of the day.

Suggestion: The leader asks the women to close their eyes, take a few deep breaths and relax. Then she says, "Imagine that you had the power to make this world just the way you wanted it to be. Now, what would that world be like? Imagine it as vividly as you can. (Pause for a little while.) Now, imagine your own life the way you would love to have it be. What would it look like? Imagine it as vividly and concretely as you can. (Another pause for a few moments.) When you are ready, open your eyes, and if you can, keep those images in the background of your mind as we go through out meeting today."

READING OF THE PURPOSE AND VISION, NINE AGREEMENTS, AND NINE QUESTIONS:

EXPLORING QUESTION SIX:

What can I imagine, and what do I want, for my flourishing, and the flourishing of all?

  First, in silence, each woman draws a simple picture or symbols of what she imagines and wants for her flourishing and the flourishing of all. Paper and crayons, or markers, or pastels, etc. are available at the Center of the circle. When everyone is done, each woman holds a ball of clay as she responds to Question Six. If she wishes, she may use her drawing as part of her sharing—or not. When each woman finishes talking, she gives the clay ball a little squeeze to leave her imprint on it, and then passes it to the next woman. When everyone has had a chance to hold the clay ball and share, the clay ball will have on it the imprints of all the women. It is placed in the Center to symbolize how we can all mold the future together.

  Finally, all the women join hands and raise them up as they look upward as if a huge dome above them on which they project with the eyes of their imagination the wants and hopes they have shared. After

a few moments gazing above at their visions, the women let go of each other's hands and each woman takes a piece of the clay ball to take home and keep in a place that will remind her of what she and the circle have imagined for the flourishing of all. The leader may close with a fitting song, prayer, or reading.

Someone volunteers to lead the next circle meeting. (Note: Not every woman has to take a turn leading, but it is important that leadership is rotated and shared by at least some of the women, so that the circle does not become dominated by one leader.) All are encouraged to take a few moments before leaving to pair up and arrange for a way to connect with each other between meetings.

CIRCLE MEETING GUIDE: SEVENTH QUESTION MEETING

Note: The leader of the seventh meeting (see below) who chooses to use the suggested rituals will need to bring a candle, matches, and a bell, small drum, or a rattle. One of these will be used as a talking object. You will also need a small plate or bowl with stones for everyone.

Welcome: Each woman says her name and why she has come, or (briefly!) anything else she chooses.

Opening Ritual: The leader lights a candle, rings a bell, or drums, or plays a musical instrument to call the group together, and leads the group in an opening moment of silence and centering or a brief meditation suited to the question of the day.

READING OF THE PURPOSE AND VISION, NINE AGREEMENTS, AND NINE QUESTIONS:

EXPLORING QUESTION SEVEN:

What concrete actions could I/we take to manifest what I/we want and need?

Suggested ritual: The leader shakes a rattle, rings a bell, or beats a drum several times. Then, in silence, each woman takes paper and pencil or pen from the Center and listens to her inner Wisdom to help her respond to this question. She writes down what she hears in the silence. It could be words, or feelings, or images, or just a knowing.

When everyone is done writing what they have "heard," the bell, drum, or rattle is passed as the talking object of the day. As each woman holds it, she responds to Question Seven, and if she wishes, shares what she heard in the silence. When everyone has had a chance to speak, the bell, drum, or rattle is passed around again, and each woman makes a sound with it to express her commitment to the actions she is willing to take.

To close, each woman takes a stone from a bowl in the Center to remind her of her commitment, and of how women can build a new and better future together, one commitment at a time, stone upon stone. The leader may offer a song, prayer, or quote to end the meeting.

Someone volunteers to lead the next circle meeting. (Note: Not every woman has to take a turn leading, but it is important that leadership is rotated and shared by at least some of the women, so that the circle does not become dominated by one leader.) All are encouraged to take a few moments before leaving to pair up and arrange for a way to connect with each other between meetings.

CIRCLE MEETING GUIDE: EIGHTH QUESTION MEETING

Note: The leader of the eighth meeting (see below) who chooses to use the suggested rituals will need to bring a candle, matches, a bell, small drum, rattle, or other musical instrument, and a good sized ball of ribbon, yarn, or string, which will be used as the talking object.

Welcome: Each woman says her name and why she has come, or (briefly!) anything else she chooses.

Opening Ritual: The leader lights a candle, rings a bell, or drums, or plays a musical instrument to call the group together, and leads the group in an opening moment of silence and centering or a brief meditation suited to the question of the day.

Suggestion: The leader asks the women to close their eyes, take a few deep breaths, and relax. Then she says, "Imagine the faces of the women and girls you know. See them before you, starting with those you know best. Look deeply, with love, into each one's eyes as you see them in your mind's eye. (Pause) Now, imagine women and girls you have never met, in places you have never been. Remember the images of women and girls in Asia, Africa, Europe, South America, and elsewhere that you have seen on television or in the newspapers and magazines. As you recall them in your mind's eye, once again imagine looking deeply with love into each one's eyes. (Pause) When you are ready, open your eyes and bring your awareness back to the room."

READING OF THE PURPOSE AND VISION, NINE AGREEMENTS, AND NINE QUESTIONS:

EXPLORING QUESTION EIGHT:

How can I live with greater connection and support with women and girls in my circles, community, and the world?

Suggested ritual: A ball of yarn, ribbon, or string is used as the talking object. Each one takes it and speaks in response to Question Eight. Then she winds the material around her hand several times. When she is finished, she passes it on to the next woman, who in turn holds it as she speaks, then winds some of the material around her hand several times, and on it goes, until everyone has had a chance to speak. When everyone is finished, all will be connected with the yarn, ribbon, or string. All sit for a few moments in silence, feeling their connection.

In closing, the leader cuts the string/yarn/ribbon between each woman. What remains around each one's wrist is to be taken home as a reminder of her commitment to make supportive connections with women and girls where she lives and out into the world.

The leader may end the meeting with a song such as "Weave, weave, weave us together" or some other appropriate song, prayer, affirmation, or reading. Someone volunteers to lead the next circle meeting. (Note:

Not every woman has to take a turn leading, but it is important that leadership is rotated and shared by at least some of the women, so that the circle does not become dominated by one leader.) All are encouraged to take a few moments before leaving to pair up and arrange for a way to connect with each other between meetings.

Note: Everyone is encouraged to come to the next meeting on the Ninth Question, which is "free choice" with the question each would choose for herself, so that all can benefit from hearing each one's choice. It would be a nice idea for each one who comes to bring some symbol of her choice as well to use as part of her sharing and put in the Center.

CIRCLE MEETING GUIDE: NINTH QUESTION MEETING

Note: The leader of the ninth meeting (see below) who chooses to use the suggested rituals will need to bring a candle, matches, a bell, small drum, rattle, or other musical instrument, and a bowl of boiled eggs for everyone, along with crayons, markers, or whatever is available with which to draw on the eggs. Add whatever the circle has decided they want for a concluding celebration!

Welcome: Each woman says her name and why she has come, or (briefly!) anything else she chooses.

Opening Ritual: The leader lights a candle, rings a bell, or drums, or plays a musical instrument to call the group together, and leads the group in an opening moment of silence and centering or a brief meditation suited to the question of the day.

Suggestion: The leader lights a candle, and invites everyone to take its light into their bodies with their eyes, then close their eyes and imagine that light filling everyone, the whole room, and then the whole world with joy and peace. Everyone breathes deeply together for a while as they imagine this Light everywhere. After a few moments of silence, the leader invites everyone to open their eyes.

READING OF THE PURPOSE AND VISION, NINE AGREEMENTS, AND NINE QUESTIONS:

EXPLORING QUESTION NINE:

Free Choice!

From a bowl of boiled eggs in the Center, each woman, in turns takes one egg, and while holding it, shares what question she has chosen to explore as part of the N.E.W. process. After she is done, she takes a marker, pen, or pencil from the Center, and draws a question mark, her initials, and if she wishes, a symbol of her question on the egg. Then she puts her egg in the bowl.

The next woman does the same thing, and so on, until everyone has had a chance to speak, and to draw their initials, a question mark, and perhaps a symbol on one of the eggs. Finally, the bowl of eggs is passed, and each woman puts her initials on every egg, so that at the end, every woman has an egg initialed by everyone in the circle as a symbol of their support, and empowerment.

This meeting ends with a celebration, perhaps planned by some of the circle members in advance. It can include music, dancing, good food, etc.

And the spiral of the N.E.W. circle begins again, going deeper and wider into each question, and empowering each woman who participates even more . . .

Someone volunteers to lead the next meeting. Not every woman has to take a turn leading, but it is important that leadership is rotated and shared by at least some of the women, so that one leader does not dominate the circle. All are encouraged to take a few moments before leaving to pair up and arrange for a way to connect with each other between meetings.

? ? ? ? ? ? ? ? ?

? ? ? ? ? ? ? ? ?

End notes: The time between this meeting and the next one, when the process begins again with Question One, is a good time to focus on

inviting women who have not yet attended to join a N.E.W. circle and try out the process for themselves. Whether it is by word of mouth only, or by announcements in a local newspaper, fliers in local places where women who might be interested stop by, or by email, let the light of your circle shine so women who need and want empowerment can find you. That is how N.E.W. will grow. And if the circle has gotten large, it would be a good idea for a couple members to start another circle, at a different time or location, so that there are more opportunities for women in your community to find a N.E.W. circle convenient for them. You have all you need to keep going and keep growing. So go for it!

Copies of these N.E.W. circle meeting guides can also be found on the website at *www.networktoempowerwomen.com* so that you can print them up and run them off for use in the circles you are a part of or choose to start.

Blessing on all you do!

LEIGH

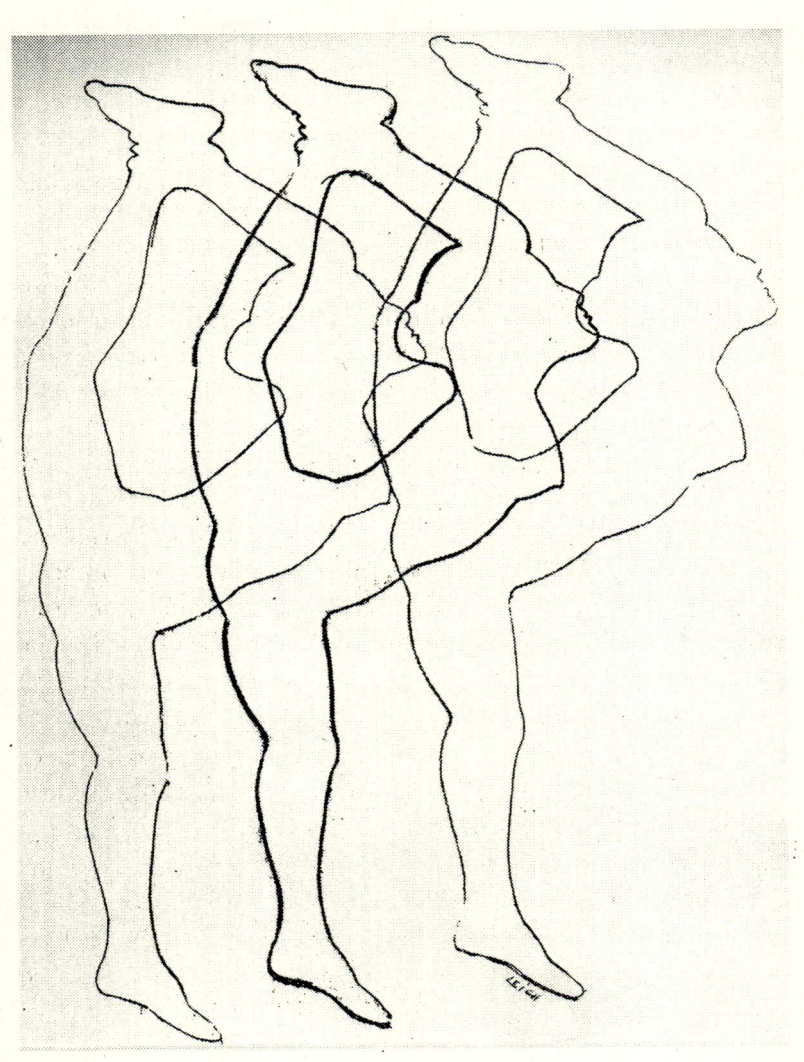

CHAPTER SIX

THE POWER OF TRUE PARTNERSHIP

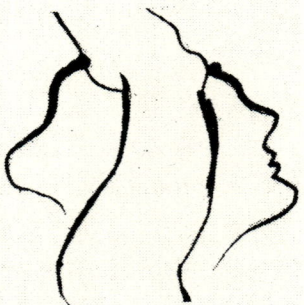

There is a question that has been lurking behind all that we have said in this book so far. "What about men?" I think this is in part because our society is largely male-focused. The vast majority of newspaper stories, headlines, movies, etc. have men as the main characters. In conversations, research shows that men usually dominate in mixed groups of men and women. The English language uses "he" and "man" for men and women, thereby rendering women invisible. Although this is changing, especially in academic circles, it still prevails in much of the media and in general usage. Even God is almost always described in male language, even though God is a Spirit, a Great Mystery, and Being itself, far beyond gender or anything we can imagine.

As a whole, women are still put in the role of minor characters in a drama and setting created by men. Women have been trained by the Status Quo to take care of men, to put them as the central characters in their lives, and to make sure they are okay. Naturally, most men like it this way. This is understandable, especially when the weight of social, legal, and religious authority supports such a setup.

Because N.E.W. has as its goal a true partnership between women and men, and because the book up to this point has been focused on women, it seems fitting that this chapter, at least, focuses on men and how they can relate as equal partners to women. Men are warmly invited to read this chapter! Women need men, just as men need women, and they must work together in a more positive way than is now the case in our world. That cannot happen unless and until more and more individual men believe that such partnership is a far better thing for them, for women, for children, and the whole world than the Status Quo. Collectively, men are just as subject to societal beliefs passed down from the past, as are women. Changes in society must be rooted and grow in individuals. This means that each man must take personal responsibility for such change, beginning with himself. Then he must put pressure on other men to relate to women as equal partners. Men can do a great deal to change each other's beliefs and actions. (Alan Johnson's book *The Gender Knot,* describes why and how this needs to take place.)

Women also need to strongly resist the present system and demand change. In fact, unless they gather up the courage to **insist** that men treat them as equal partners, it is unlikely that most men will change. In order to do this, women need each other to support and help them in this effort. (That is why N.E.W. circles and similar women's support groups are so important.) While there are some men who are open, fair, and willing to change, there are many who are not. Like people who are addicted, they will not change unless it is **less** painful to change than keep things going as they are. When women make it difficult enough for men to keep the Status Quo in place, partnership will become a real possibility.

Both men and women need to stop being in denial about the need for change in their personal relationships, and in the structures of society. Denial is one of the chief symptoms of addiction, and it is safe to say that a great many people of both genders are attached to the Status Quo, because it seems more comfortable not to "rock the boat." If the boat is not rocked, however, it is clear that it just might capsize, and that is a far worse alternative than the discomfort and hard work it takes to create change. In short, men and women must work together to create equal partnership where they live and work and play. Their strategies may be different, but the goal is the same.

In the end, it is **only** true partnership in homes and in society that will change the mess we are in. Just as putting a drop of color in a jar of water changes the character of the water, so too, each man and woman's change in beliefs and actions will change the whole picture. When enough men and women are living their lives in every arena as true partners, it will become clear that Status Quo has outlived whatever usefulness it might have had, and it will be consigned to the dustbin of history.

But what does true partnership look like? We need to have a clear picture of it before we can decide we want it, believe it can happen, and then act to make it happen. The first place to look is nearest to us, in our homes. Equal partnership in the home is the foundation of equal partnership in the rest of society. It is, perhaps, the most difficult place to create it, because it is in our families that we are shaped as children with the beliefs that will determine the rest of our lives. Most of us were not brought up in homes where true partnership prevailed. We carry unconscious beliefs and habits of the heart with us into the homes we establish. It takes careful attention and determined effort to find a different way for our selves.

Moreover, it is in our homes that we live together most intimately, and are most vulnerable. It is in homes that men and women most often rub each other the wrong way, and get into ugly power struggles and habits of mutual destruction. It is in homes that most violence and abuse of children and women takes place, and where some men are also abused. It is also in homes that the daily decisions that shape our lives are made.

On the other hand, it is in homes that true partnership begins, and is possible. When there is such true partnership, it is a powerful force for good. There is no violence or abuse in such homes. There is a spirit of cooperation, mutual respect, fairness, honesty, and loving-kindness instead. Everyone in such a home is much happier than in a home where domination and control over others is the prevailing mode of operation. I know of such homes, where men and women have created true partnership. They are like lighthouses shedding a beacon of light to others caught in the tempest of the so-called "battle of the sexes. " Such battle is caused by the effort of one party to dominate the other, subtly or obviously. This is the cause of all battles, in the home and beyond it. That is why, when there is peace instead of battle in the homes of the world, there is far more likely to be peace in the world beyond the home.

The battle of the sexes is based on the false belief that men and women are opposites. How often do you not hear the expression "the opposite sex."? Nonsense! Men and women have far more in common as human beings than they have differences because they are one gender or the other. They are humans first, and men and women second. They are complementary, not opposite. The differences between them, which interestingly enough, are defined very differently in various societies around the world, are no reason to treat each other as "opposite." Males and females are not so different that there is no chance of really understanding each other. Even biologically, the differences are small compared to the sameness. Men and women have the same basic internal anatomy and external bodies except for the specific sexual differences. Both are fully human, fully persons, with brains and bodies that function · far more similarly than differently.

The differences have been exaggerated by the Domination System of belief, because if the other is so different, maybe not even fully human, than it is alright to treat them very differently than you yourself would want to be treated. This is the belief that underlies racism as well as sexism. A horrible example of this belief is the effort by certain authorities in the early history of the Church to deny that women have souls and are as fully the Image of God as men are.

The situation in some parts of the Church to this day speaks of the lingering effects of this false and damaging belief. Dorothy Sayers, a well-known British author, wrote a book in the 20th century entitled *Are Women Human?* There were and are reasons for the title! In the history of the United States, slavery was justified by the belief that Africans didn't have souls like white folk. I wonder if that belief is altogether dead!

In other religions and cultures as well, the differences between men and women are emphasized in order to keep women separate and limited. The society of Saudi Arabia is one example. Many more examples could be cited. In each of them, the differences between men and women, or between ethnic groups, or tribes, or classes, are used to justify injustice and oppression.

On the other side of the picture is the Golden Rule, which has its parallel in every major world religion and culture. "Do unto others as you would have them do unto you. " This ancient, universal Wisdom, if followed in all relationships, would rid the world of most of its sorrow and tragedy.

True partnership in the home is based on the Golden Rule. Both husband and wife treat each other as they would want to be treated. If there are sacrifices to be made, they share them equally. For instance, if there is a couple with children, and both the father and mother have abilities they want to exercise by working outside the home, both do all they can to make that possible. The traditional marriage requires the woman to give years of her life taking care of the house and children, and get no pay or financial security in return. Often, this demanding task is not even considered "real work," and women who do it are made to feel that being "just a housewife" is second best. The man is the sole support of the family in this arrangement, and gives years working long hours, often at unsatisfying work, to earn sufficient money for the family. He is paid for his work, and thus what he does has more status in society. Nevertheless, this traditional model for marriage is not working for the vast majority of married couples with children these days. That's why such families are now a shrinking minority. If both husband and wife freely and gladly choose this model, that is fine, but it is the fact that it is freely and gladly chosen by *both* of them which makes it compatible with true partnership. It is crucial that both men and women demand that the task of caring for home and children be an honored profession, recognized as exceedingly demanding, extremely valuable for the good of society, and therefore rewarded not only with high respect and status, but with monetary rewards and social security as well. After all, if men and women do not choose to do this task, and do it well, and if it is not far more highly regarded and rewarded in society than it presently is, the future for our children looks bleak. Rather than making the priorities of the workplace dominate the demands of home life, it should be the other way around.

In an economy which presently requires that many families have two incomes just to make ends meet, the luxury of one spouse being able to devote full time to family and home is unfortunately more and more rare. Given this state of affairs, it is necessary for the man and woman to equally share in the work of the home since they are sharing in the work required to earn a living. This is what happens in true partnership. I know more and more couples who are doing this, whether they have children or not, and they are a lot happier than couples which do not fairly and kindly share in the necessary tasks of life together. When I talk to them about how and why they live as true partners, they say things like this: (These statements are based on actual conversations with real-life couples who have worked hard on living together as equal partners.)

Men: It's not that hard! There are a lot of advantages to being partners. I don't feel the burden of earning a living is all up to me. My wife doesn't feel the burden of taking care of a house and children is all up to her. I just think it's natural and right to treat her fairly. I wouldn't want to have a job and have to come home and do most of the chores or child-care. So why should I make her do this?

Women: Really caring about each other is the key, instead of just thinking of "me." We are partners to help each other in life, in small ways and big ways. I help him so he can use his abilities out in the world, and he helps me so I can do the same. We each want the other person to flourish—to be all they can be.

Men: It means a lot to me that my wife gives her blessing to my doing things I love in my free time, like being outdoors, hiking, fishing, or whatever. When I am not made to feel guilty for filling my needs, I am much happier sharing in the household tasks. And I think it is nonsense to think that dusting or mowing or laundry or cooking are somehow "women's work" or "men's work." I can do any of these things perfectly well, if I want to. And so can she.

Women: I appreciate that my husband gives his blessing to what I need and love to do too. He doesn't expect me to take care of him and the children while neglecting myself. I call that loving-kindness, which is even more basic than fairness. You can get into arguments about what is fair, and your relationship can start to feel like a business contract. But when he and I are both focusing on being concerned for each other's welfare, then we can be real friends and partners.

Men: I don't expect my wife to meet all my needs, and she doesn't expect me to meet all of hers. We have a strong sense of who we are, and we don't cling to each other to fill a big empty hole inside ourselves. We know we are worthwhile as human beings apart from what we do or what other people think of us. Our spiritual beliefs give us our sense of worthiness and meaning. So we can be partners, but still independent. A lot of guys think of marriage as a ball and chain. I bet a lot of women do too! But it only feels like that when you *use* each other to meet your own needs. As partners, we try not to use each other. We try to support each other and bring out the best in each other.

Women: You have to know who you are apart from your husband.
You have to have a strong sense of yourself and trust both yourself and him. Faithfulness to each other is basic. And so is real respect. We respect each other's needs, each other's ideas, each other's work, and each other's abilities. We see our relationships as a covenant, a sacred agreement to be here for one another through thick and thin.

That is the foundation. With a strong foundation, you can remodel your relationship as needed, because things do change! Even though part of our relationship is just taking care of business in the fairest possible way, it is a deep friendship on another level. That would not be possible if he called all the shots and I felt unfairly treated and disrespected, as if all that mattered was what he wanted. We avoid friendships with couples like that. We deliberately chose as our best friends couples who have the same values of partnership that we do. After all, it is pretty tough to do what we are doing in a society where it is still the exception rather than the rule. We need all the help we can get from other like-minded people!

Men: It isn't true that work is the most rewarding thing in life. If you have children, raising them is the most rewarding and important thing you can do. Why leave it to the women? Children need us men. We have different strengths to offer them, different things to teach them. They grow up so fast! Why waste those precious hours you could be with them and your partner working for some institution that uses you up, and will just go right on trucking, with or without you. You are much more needed at home than in any job!

Men who get their whole sense of worth by what they do, or how much they earn are in big trouble. You can always lose your job or have a pay cut. But no one can take away your worth as a good husband, father, and partner in the home. You will always have that if you make it important in your life. What's more, for a lot of men, work is not that enjoyable, especially when it demands so much time and energy. It can just suck the life out of you and use up this one precious life you have. Men created this system that does this to us, and we would be a lot better off if we changed it. Who says forty or more hours a week is the only way to structure things? What's wrong with thirty, so more people have jobs, and parents can share equally in raising their children with the free time they would have? And when the kids are grown up, you have all this free time to enjoy doing what you love most, or exploring new things, helping out in the community, or whatever.

Women: I love the fact that my husband clearly thinks I am even more important to him than his job. He is certainly more important to me than my job. And so are the children, and our life together. I love my job, though, and I am glad I can work outside the house without getting all stressed out, because my husband is a real partner. We have learned that both homework and world-work are most rewarding when we see them as serving each other, and children, and society.

Men: It isn't just about making money. Money and a job are not what make us happy. People who think money and their work are the most important things are people who have a big hole inside themselves these things can't fill. It's happy, loving relationships, and knowing you are making the world a better place by what you do and how you live that makes life really worth living.

Women: The best partners are those who are willing to sacrifice for each other, and make sacrifices together for the good of their children, if they have any, and the society they live in. A lot of women are understandably nervous about being asked to make sacrifices. They feel they have been asked to do most of the sacrificing in society. They have sacrificed the rewards of using their abilities in society outside of the home for a long time. They have sacrificed their time for other people's needs so much, they hardly know what they want and need. They sacrifice their husbands and sons to wars created by men. They sacrifice the best years of their lives to a husband who rejects them for someone else.

But the kind of sacrifice made in a true partnership is very different. It is not forced by society, or by anyone. It is freely and gladly made in a relationship in which the other person is also making sacrifices for you. That is what makes the whole sacrifice thing work.

Men: Men make a huge sacrifice when they give up the rewards of time at home, with their children and wives, or with good friends, in order to prove their superiority by how hard they work. Guys often have bragging contests about who works hardest. If they only realized the pleasure they are giving up! Such men have hardly any friends, and a pretty lousy home life. That's not a smart choice!

It isn't wise for men to sacrifice their lives in each other's wars either. Why give your one special life up for a system that makes violence the main way to settle conflict? We have not spent one tenth the money and effort on figuring out how to settle things without violence, as we have on the war and weapons machine. It's a huge and needless sacrifice we are making. Trying to be the most supposedly powerful is the root of many of the problems we have. Whether it is one country over or another, or one person over others, it is the same stupid domination game going on.

When men realize the huge price they pay by trying to control their wives, or other people, we will stop doing it. It just makes us feel anxious, because we know deep down that our control can be challenged, and we could lose it, whether it's our wives or our children or other people we are trying to control. It is a lot more rewarding, and less stressful, to co-operate with others, men and women, than try to be top dog all the time. That's no fun! Why would men want to keep feeling lonely, stressed, and threatened deep down? Why wouldn't men want to enjoy the huge satisfaction and pleasure of good relationships with women, with children, and other men? So many of us were brought up by fathers who didn't live this way. It hurt us a lot. Why keep hurting, and passing on the hurt to the next generation? It doesn't make any sense.

Women: True partnership is about co-operation, harmony, and balance, not about competing with each other.

Men: Well, men seem to be by nature competitive, at least in this society. Competition isn't necessarily bad, if it 's the right kind of competition. It might be a good thing if we competed with each other for who was the best partner in their home, who was the best father to their children, who balanced their work and the rest of their life the best, who had the most pleasurable and satisfying life. I think it would soon be obvious to most of us that having lots of money is much less rewarding than being a good partner, father, and a balanced person with time for what is really important.

* * *

This dialogue is a composite of the things men and women have said to me as we talked about true partnership. Most of what they said was about personal relationships and home life. It could be equally applied to any people who live together and are making a home and life with one another. A lot of what men and women said to me is a description of genuine love as it is lived out in the nitty-gritty of life. It is working for an increasing number of couples and families. That gives me great hope for the future.

There is still the matter of true partnership beyond the home to consider. Much of what men and women said in the dialogue above applies there as well. Wherever men and women work together in society, true partnership demands mutual fairness, respect, honesty, and trying to bring out the best in one another. That goes a very long way in bridging differences and creating balance and harmony.

But what does it actually look like out there in the world? Very, very few businesses, government institutions, religious institutions, or educational institutions have men and women in roughly equal numbers in all positions from "top to bottom," working together as partners. Women as a whole occupy the majority of the bottom positions in arenas in which they have any part at all. Most of the cleaning, child-care, elder-care, nursing, teaching of children, clerking, waiting tables, and the like, is done by women. In nearly every society in the world, men hold most of the top decision making positions with money and status. In the middle, depending on the arena of society, there is a mixture of men and women, though not often an equal mixture, whether it comes to numbers, or working conditions, or pay. This is what we see. Is it what we want? Is it best for any society? For men, women, and children? For the planet? I think it is obvious that the answer is a resounding, "NO!"

Lynn Grabhorn tells us, as quoted in a previous chapter, that the first step towards getting what we want is to know clearly what we do NOT WANT. Then, from that, we can see clearly what we DO WANT. That gives us a pretty straightforward way to see what true partnership would look like.

As men and women who want to live together as partners, we do NOT WANT the Status Quo:

1. We do **not want** men and women segregated into "blue collar" and "pink collar" ghettos in the workplace. All work, if it is worth doing at all, is worth doing well by a man or a woman. Women don't necessarily make the best secretaries and nurses. Men do not necessarily make the best carpenters and mechanics. We experience these things as true because we believe certain stereotypes. When a man or a woman challenges the stereotype by doing something well that he or she is supposedly not capable of, the stereotype, or belief, starts to break down, and something new can happen. Look around, and you will see many examples of this.

2. We do **not want** unequal pay and working conditions for men and women. Fair is fair. Women's work is as valuable as men's in the home and in society, and both genders should be fairly compensated for their work in equal measure, and be treated on the job with equal respect.
3. We do **not want** sexual harassment and hurdles for women in the work place, or anywhere else. These things are signs of the lack of true partnership, which implies mutual respect and fair treatment of women by men when they work together.
4. We do **not want** schools, churches, mosques, temples, synagogues, businesses, governmental organizations, professional organizations, military organizations, health organizations, the media, publishing, or any other societal institutions run by mostly men. This creates a one-sided, male-dominated, limited perspective and pool of wisdom and talent. Given the state of the world today, we must have the perspective, wisdom, and talent of women in equal numbers at all levels of these institutions. Men and women need to share power, and make it truly life-giving, focused on the flourishing of all, not just one segment of society, one gender, one race, one social group, one geographical area, or one country.

It is perfectly clear. What we DO WANT is a big change in the Status Quo. What we DO WANT is equal opportunity, fair treatment, and respectful mutual working together to bring out each other's best qualities as men and women, in every single arena of life.

What we DO WANT is a world in which women and men work together in mutually empowering ways. The Status Quo is organized so that in most organizations a few people (usually men) at the top have some kind of control over everyone beneath them. A pyramid best symbolizes this system, and we all remember where pyramids originated and what kind of society that was! Isn't it time we left the ways of the Pharaohs behind?

Organizations which have been experimenting with working together in mutually empowering ways, best symbolized by a circle, are finding that things go much better. Everyone's ideas are available for the good of the organization, because everyone is listened to respectfully. The burden for making the organization run well doesn't rest on the CEO and few of his cohorts. This new model for running things is catching on in many places in the world because it works so much better than the pyramid model.

True partnership between men and women is fostered by the circle, not by the pyramid! (See Christina Baldwin's book *Calling the Circle,* for more on this.)

Only true partnership in every arena has the potential to turn things around to create a peaceful, flourishing world. The evidence lies all around us, impossible to deny. Women's valuable knowledge and abilities can complement men's in a way that will make this world much, much better. Isn't it time we believe true partnership is possible, and desirable? If we do, we will have the chance to experience how good true partnership can be for everyone everywhere. The great, innate life-giving power of women, in partnership with men, is the only thing that can save our world, humanly speaking, from its present disastrous course. Half of the human race is waiting to have its wisdom and abilities fully unleashed for the welfare of the planet. The bird that is humanity needs both of its wings to fly into a bright future. This is what WE WANT! It is important to focus on this, not on what we don't want.

With our focus on what we WANT, as men and as women who care about the world as well as our personal lives, we need to realize the power of our beliefs to get what we want. I understand a belief to be a combination of concept and conviction. Concept is thought, conviction is feeling. Together, the two form beliefs that, if strong enough, can change the Status Quo. As we have already seen in this book, beliefs can be discarded, and beliefs can be chosen. We as humans have the innate and wonderful power to do this. The best question to ask to get in touch with this power is "What do I **want** to believe?"

It is interesting that the best, highest, and noblest beliefs of the human race, as mirrored in the greatest, most lasting religions and philosophies of our history, support the wisdom of true partnership, peace, harmony, balance, and loving kindness. Here, for example, are various version of the "Golden Rule," taken from a North American Interfaith Network poster presented to the United Nations in 2001. A statement made at the presentation said that the existence of the Golden Rule in every faith was evidence of a Global Ethic that transcends nations, civilizations, and religions, and that it should be obeyed by all nations. No persons or societies should exempt themselves from the demands of the Universal "Golden Rule."

Here are its various versions:

- We are as much alive as we keep the earth alive. (Aboriginal spirituality)
- Lay not on any soul a load that you would not wish to be laid upon you, and desire not for anyone the things you would not desire for yourselves. (Baha'I Faith)
- Treat not others in ways that you yourself would find hurtful. (Buddhism)
- In everything, do to others as you would have them to do you; for this is the law and the prophets. (Christianity)
- One word which sums up the basis of all good conduct . . . loving-kindness. Do not do to others what you do not want done to yourself. (Confucianism)
- This is the sum of duty: do not do to others what would cause pain if done to you. (Hinduism)
- Not one of you truly believes until you wish for others what you wish for yourself. (Islam)
- One should treat all creatures in the world as one would like to be treated. (Jainism)
- What is hateful to you, do not do to your neighbor. This is the whole Torah; all the rest is commentary. (Judaism)
- I am a stranger to no one; and no one is a stranger to me. Indeed, I am a friend to all. (Sikhism)
- Regard your neighbor's gain as your own gain, and your neighbor's loss as your own loss. (Taoism)
- Do not do unto others whatever is injurious to yourself. (Zoroastrianism)

It is not difficult to see how each and all of these religious precepts apply clearly to the relationships between men and women, as well as between races, nations, and humanity and all other creatures. I believe Divine Wisdom has implanted these ideals in our hearts for our flourishing. We can choose the beliefs that are rooted in this Divine Universal Wisdom, and discard the beliefs of the Status Quo in our various societies which contradict them. (Ways of doing this have already been explored in the chapter on Real Power.) I want to encourage men, in particular, to use their real power to discard whatever beliefs they may have that get in the way of true partnership, and choose beliefs that promote partnership instead. Each man must determine for himself what beliefs to discard, and what beliefs to choose to live out in his life.

Then, and this is absolutely essential, men need to challenge the beliefs and acts of other men which are incompatible with true partnership between men and women. We women need you men to do this. You know, as men, that there are many men who will not listen to a woman, when they will listen to another man. It is you who must have the courage and conviction to challenge men who demean women, shut them out, shut them up, or violate their trust.

The whole Domination System, the Status Quo, is a handed-down set of beliefs that influence men to view women as inferior, and themselves as having the right to shape society as they please. There is no point in you, as a man, feeling guilty about this. You did not invent the system. It was handed down to you by the generations of men who have gone before you, and even by women who went along with the Status Quo. A guilt trip is a dead end. So is blaming yourself or others. What is needed instead, is for you to act out of deliberately chosen, positive beliefs to challenge the Status Quo with your words and deeds. Don't be silent when demeaning comments are made in your presence about women. Speak up to promote women for positions in your workplace when you have a chance. Interrupt the flow of business as usual when it is clear that business as usual is preventing true partnership.

Plant seeds of doubt about whether things as they are really *need* to be this way. Plant the seeds of different and better possibilities. Don't be afraid to make other people, men especially, uncomfortable. The degree of their discomfort shows the degree of your power to challenge what is going on. By your words and actions you can help the men around you realize that things could be different. For instance, if you decide to work part time, and care for the children and home part time, you will make that possibility real in many men's minds, and the usual way of doing this will begin to seem less inevitable. If you decide to make a woman a full and equal partner in your firm or business, you challenge the prevailing idea that a woman should serve in a subordinate capacity. Even little remarks you make can cause the men around you to examine their beliefs and attitudes.

The Domination System of the Status Quo survives only because men pressure each other to conform to its beliefs and way of doing things. Solidarity among men is the main bulwark of this system. That is why men are made to feel like "sissies" or "not a real man" when they speak or act in ways that don't conform to the system. It takes courage to risk the disapproval and even hostility of men who don't want change and don't like your challenges. But you as a man have lots of courage, and you can do it. Men are willing to literally die to defend their country, their homes, and their loved ones. How much better to put that wonderful courage and ability to work challenging beliefs which keep this world a place where violence and cruelty are condoned, and everyone suffers terribly because of it: men, women, children, and animals.

Surely men can risk ruffling the feathers of another man by suggesting in one way or another that human welfare is more important than war, that harmony is better than hate, and that men and women make good partners! As Allan Johnson says in the conclusion to his excellent book *The Gender Knot,* "We become part of the long tradition of people who have dared to make a difference—to look at things as they are, to imagine something better, and to plant seeds of change in themselves, in others, and in the world."(p. 253)

It is true, thank goodness, that men are already doing this. But "a few good men" are not enough. We need many, many more men who will have the courage and character to challenge the Domination System every single day, in some way or other, big or small. This is how change happens. With women also doing this in their own way, change is inevitable!

I do not underestimate the difficulty of this effort at this point, however. I believe we stand at a crucial crossroads in human history. We are the crossover generation, the bridge between a past dominated by the false use of power, and a future that can flourish with the true and right use of power. It is up to us. There is no one else. We are it. And we need each other's help. Men especially need the help of other like-minded men if they are to have the support and resources required to challenge the Status Quo, when so much is invested in it.

When the start of N.E.W. circles was announced at a church service I attended a while ago, a man came up to me and said wistfully, "But—don't we men need empowering too?" My first reaction was "Are you kidding? You are the ones with most of the power in the world!" Of course, I didn't say this aloud. And on second thought, I agreed with him. The kind of power men as a whole have used is false power, not true power. It is the innate power humans have, turned towards seeking power over others. It is fear-based power, and therefore weak at the core. True power is life giving, and strong at the core.

"Yes," I replied, "men do need empowerment. They need to realize what true power is, and how to use it rightly in partnership with women for the welfare of the world. I am going to give what you said careful thought." And I have. I propose the coming together of men in a network of circles that could be called M.E.N.—**Men's Empowerment Network.** These circles should use the same basic format and Nine Agreements for the process of the meeting as N.E.W. circles do. There is nothing about them that excludes men.

It should be remembered that for eons, men in Native American and other Original People tribes throughout the world have used a process very much like this one when they gathered in council. These were men who were strong, skillful, and good at the traditional "manly" arts of hunting, fishing, and warfare. The circle process worked well for them, as well as for the women of those ancient tribes, for thousands of years, and it can work well for men today. All men need to do is give it a chance. Meeting together using the same process used in N.E.W. circles is a good way of doing it. The strong structure provides a way for men to interact within a framework that allows for genuine sharing, and prevents anyone from dominating. Many men are hungry for this kind of interaction. (For more about this, see Baldwin's book *Calling the Circle: the First and Future Culture* for information on how circles have worked and are now working, and other resources for using them in various settings.)

As you look at the guides for the meetings in the chapter "The Power of Experience," just change the words "women" to "men" and they should apply to M.E.N. circles with ease. The Nine Agreements really do not need any other changes.

The Nine Questions can be used with some minor modifications. Here are the ones I recommend:

Question One: What am I grateful to have survived and accomplished so far? Who and/or what has empowered me, and how? (Keep in mind what true power is for this question.)

Question Two: What damaging, false beliefs about myself as a man, and about men and women in general, do I want to get rid of?

What positive, helpful beliefs about myself, and men and women in general, do I want to choose and live out in my life?

Question Three: How have I found and followed my own unique Inner Authority as a human being? How will I continue to do so?

Question Four: What are the spiritual practices and resources that empower me?

Question Five: As a man, what obstacles have I encountered to using my power in a positive way? What obstacles to using their innate power do I observe women encounter? (Always keep in mind the definition of power in the Vision and Goals read at the start of the meeting.) What are some effective strategies for dealing with these obstacles, for me, and in behalf of women?

Question Six: What can I imagine, and what do I want for my flourishing and the flourishing of all? What are the noblest and best possibilities?

Question Seven: What concrete actions could I/we as men take to make what I/we imagine and want for the welfare of all actually happen?

Question Eight: How can I/we live with greater connection and support with boys and like-minded men in my/our community, in our society, and in the world? How can I/we live as true partners with the women in my/our life, our society, and in the world?

Question Nine: Your choice!

The suggested rituals at the beginning, end, and for exploring each of these questions can, of course, be modified by the men in the circle to suit themselves. But it is important in M.E.N. groups to use the same process as described in the N.E.W. meeting guides, including the Nine Questions (modified as suggested above) and the Nine Agreements. By using this ancient circle process, men will come to experientially understand the difference between false and true power. That is the only way to really understand it. Talking about it is not enough. For men especially, socially conditioned as they are, there is no substitute for a process like the one used in N.E.W. circles to help them realize what true power actually feels like and how it works. Then, they can apply this experience in the rest of their lives, and things will change for the better.

Should any men choose to create M.E.N. groups, please let me know via e-mail or on the N.E.W. website, which is mentioned several times in this book and at the end in the Resource Appendix. I would like to hear how the process works with men.

After men have gone through the whole cycle of Nine Questions, whether they do it in nine weeks, or nine months, they are equipped to meet with a N.E.W. circle of women now and then, by mutual agreement. These meetings should be in addition to the regular ongoing N.E.W. women's circles, and M.E.N.'s circles. Both women and men in our society need to be together in the way made possible by the circle process and questions. But first, they need to get used to this way of operating separately, so that when they come together, there is no danger of slipping into bad old habits of interaction, in which men generally dominate a conversation.

Once men and women have gotten used to equal and respectful kind of sharing and silent listening to one another in their separate circles, they can meet in a way that helps create an effective way of being together as true partners. Circles in which both men and women are present should make sure that everyone knows in advance that this will be happening, so that if any man or woman doesn't want to be with the other gender in this setting, they can skip the meeting. At this point in history, a lot of women are still not willing to open up in front of a man, because of their negative experiences. Some men may have the same issue. For those who are ready, meeting together can be a way of learning how to relate to each other as true partners. Nothing but good can come of this. Such experience readily spills over into other parts of our lives, and creates a powerful impetus for positive change.

I am personally eager to be part of just such an experiment, and am eager to hear from any of you, the readers, who decide to try it as well. You know by now how to contact me!

My dream is that there will not only be N.E.W. circles everywhere, but M.E.N. circles too, until the day when neither is needed because the kind of world wide partnership-society envisioned in this book will be an every day reality.

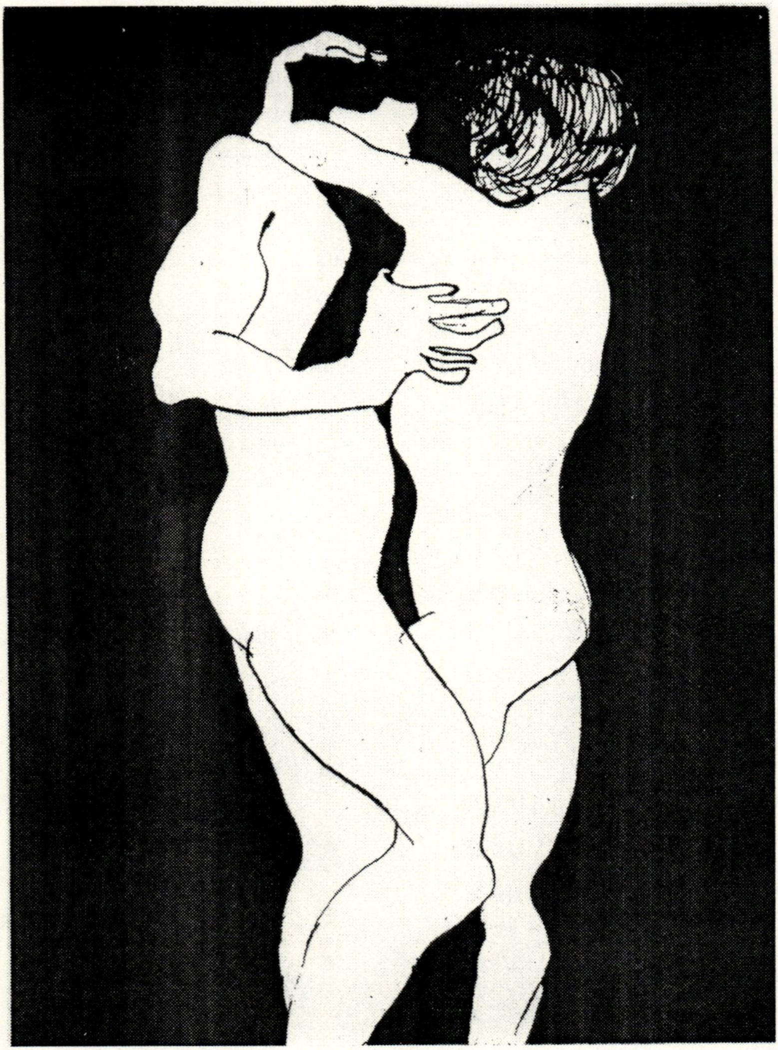

CHAPTER SEVEN

FUTURE POWER

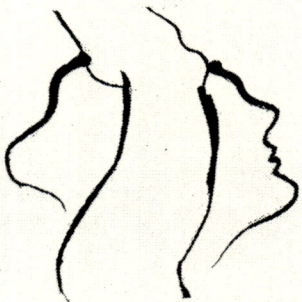

The future of this world, if it is to have one, lies in the hands of today's children. If we are to have the kind of future we envision, children must flourish, and we must do all in our power to see that they do. How can we expect our world to thrive if our children are not thriving now? The kind of partnership society between men and women envisioned by N.E.W. is not possible unless children NOW are greatly valued, and are guided to become men and women who can live together as true partners.

Many people will say how precious children are. But the Status Quo obviously does not truly value them. It treats them more like a commodity than a sacred trust. Look. Listen. If the welfare of children were a top priority, wouldn't things be very different? Would war be an option? Look what it does to children. Would poverty as the product of an unjust global economic system be an option? Look what it does to the great majority of children all over the world. Would violence in the home be an option? Look how it affects children. Would we allow the media and music we now allow? Look how it affects children. Would we continue to support work demands that keep parents from spending the time with their children they need? Look how it affects children.

Look how all of this affects children!

I read a novel a while ago based on the idea that there was an unexpected biological mutation in the whole human species. It was no longer possible to have children. No woman got pregnant. At first, people didn't notice. But as the birth rate plummeted everywhere, it dawned on people that the human race was in serious trouble. Can you imagine the reaction? How would we feel, how would we act, if we knew there would be no more children?

Children are our most precious Divine gift. They carry the seed of the future. More than that, they bring great treasures into our lives: joy, love, hope, meaning, laughter, a sense of wonder, play, purpose, and a lot of expanding of our perspective and abilities. Someone once said, "Every baby is God's vote of confidence in the human race." Isn't it time we acted in a way worthy of that confidence? Isn't it time we insisted that society cherish its children as its most important natural resource? If they are not, who or what is?

Every child is also a Divine teacher. I am sure I have learned more from my children and grandchildren than they have from me. They have taught me to live intensely and joyfully in the present moment. They have showed me how to enjoy little things I take for granted; the taste of a cookie, the squirrels chasing each other around a tree trunk, a drop of dew shining on a spider web. They have reminded me of the value of being open, teachable, asking questions. They have stretched my soul with the depth of some of those questions, and made me cry with others. "Where does God live?" "Can I fly to the moon?" "Why do those families have to live on the street?" "How come people want to kill each other?" "Do dogs go to heaven when they die?" They have demonstrated perfect lack of prejudice, and breath-taking honesty. They have given me unconditional forgiveness and love and appreciation.

I could go on for pages, naming the gifts children bring into our lives. They shape us, requiring that we become better people if we are to take good care of them. We shape them too, and we can teach them to hate and fear, or we can cultivate their innate love and sense of fair play. Because they are vulnerable and inexperienced in life, we need to be their guardians and guides. What an awesome responsibility this is.

The first and most important part of our responsibility is to love them, whether we have children of our own, or not. Everyone can love at least one child. A lot of children need that love. A good way to describe the kind of love children need is to see it as composed of at least these three elements: attention, appreciation, and assistance.

First, pay attention to children in your life. You can't love someone who you are ignoring! That is why attention is so crucial, and without it, children malfunction. It takes time, energy, and a real desire to know children to pay attention to them—positive attention, that is. When we shine the sun of loving attention on the children around us, they thrive like plants do in sunlight. We, in turn, learn much about them and from them. My youngest daughter remembers a friend of mine who was one of the only adults she recalls who talked to her like a real person when she was little. To this day, that friend has a special place in her heart. It is so easy to be pre-occupied with less important things: our jobs, our problems, money, ideas, projects, or other people. But when we pay attention to children, we are really loving them, and creating a better present and future for them and ourselves.

Attention is the gateway to appreciation. Many children will misbehave because they feel ignored. They want attention, and if they don't get it, they will do something to attract it, even if it is the negative attention of scolding or even punishment. At least their existence is being acknowledged! But when attention is combined with appreciation, it is magical in its positive effect on children.

This is not the same thing as false flattery. Children know when you are being real. Watch for things to appreciate about what they say or do, and their attitudes and perspectives. Let them know how much you enjoy them, and what you appreciate about them as unique little persons. You don't always have to put it in words. Your look, your smile, your hug, can say more than words.

Along with attention and appreciation, assistance is something all children need. It is easy to see how children need assistance with things like tying shoelaces, reaching something high up, learning to brush their teeth, and the like. It is harder, but important, to see assistance as helping children when they are in the grip of anger, frustration, or grief. Listen to their feelings and let them vent in a non-hurtful way. Then help them with positive alternatives for dealing with their feelings and the situation that they are reacting to.

Let us say Johnny hits Jane because she has a toy he wants and she won't give it to him. To scold him is negative attention. Instead, separate them, and talk to Johnny alone, asking him to tell why he is angry. Then suggest something else he can play with, or another way to approach Jane about the toy. This is attentive and positive assistance. By acknowledging that feelings are okay, and showing them how not to be controlled by them, we teach children important life skills. If they know we love them, even when they do things we don't like, they will be much more likely to accept our assistance and follow our guidance.

As adults, it is also our job to protect children from harm. The most obvious way is to teach them what dangers in the environment to avoid: going into deep water without an adult nearby; playing with fire; avoiding creatures whose bites are poisonous; and other dangers. We must also teach them how to protect themselves against the harm others can do to them. This means encouraging them to speak out when they feel threatened, to have the freedom to say no and run away from adults whose actions don't feel good, to refuse to keep "secrets" even when threatened, to let trusted adults know where they are, and so on.

What is needed just as much is to protect children from the negative messages in the media around them. What values, what beliefs, and what examples of how to live are they being exposed to? Are they the values we want them to live by? If not, we need to expose them instead to the best beliefs, the highest values and ideals, by choosing for them what books, what T.V. and radio programs, what videos, what computer games, what magazines, and what music they absorb into their minds and hearts.

Children are like sponges. If we love them, we will not let them soak up poison. If we are too busy to protect them in these ways, we are too busy. The power to shape the future will be in their hands someday. Now, they are in our hands, and therefore, so is the future they will create. They need contact with us, and need to hear us talking about the positive beliefs and ideals we cherish. TV's, radios, and computers in children's bedrooms insure that you will not be able to protect them while they are young from negative influences. Much of what they see and hear in the media these days hardly supports true partnership between men and women and the ideals that support a flourishing future for the world. To protect children is to be vigilant about what they are exposed to.

The hardest part of our responsibility in raising children who will be able to create a flourishing future is to *be* what we want *them* to be. Our words have far less influence on them than our actions. If we want them to be fair and kind, we must be. If we want them to value males and females equally, so must we. If we want them to strive for peaceful solutions, so must we. If we don't want them to drink alcohol, smoke, or abuse drugs, neither must we. This is how they help us to become the very best people we are capable of being. They look to us as examples. By our example today, we are powerfully shaping the future that is in their hands.

One of the best ways to teach children the values and beliefs we have found life giving and positive is through stories. Lessons and values taught in stories stick much better than lectures from adults. There are a lot of stories out there written for children. Look at them carefully. Do they teach that violence is a solution to conflict? How do they depict the nature and roles of males and females? What values underlie the story? What beliefs shape what happens? And how does all that fit with what you want your children to believe and value, and how you want them to live their lives?

Another wonderful way to help children learn the beliefs and values you want them to have is to make up stories with them. Together, you can create your very own unique stories that reflect your ideals and values in a way that is interesting and fun. Children love to have you write out their story ideas. They love to talk about them and create them with you. They love to draw illustrations for them. This process invites the kind of exploring of underlying beliefs that is the essence of guiding our children. Creating together creates strong bonds, and what you create has Future Power. So—create!

To inspire you, here is a story I created with my grandchildren:

THE FUTURE FOR WOMEN - A N.E.W. BOOK

THE DRAGON THAT CHANGED

Once upon a time, in the magical space between yesterday, today, and tomorrow, there lived on an island in the Inland Sea a huge, green-scaled, iron-clawed, fire-breathing dragon with the unlikely name of Forget-Me-Not. She was born by breaking out of a huge golden egg laid by her dragon mother in a dark cave deep in the heart of the high green hills at the center of the island. She lived there long, lonely day after long, lonely night, with nothing to keep her company but the huge treasure trove that lay on the stony floor of her cave.

Now as you might have guessed, Forget-Me-Not was a most unhappy dragon. Not only was she as lonely as could be. She was angry and bitter too. For she brooded on the stories her mother had told, before she died and sank hissing into the bottom of the sea. They were stories about a time when dragons were a happy, bright red color, and didn't need iron claws or hard green scales to protect their bodies. They smiled and laughed instead of breathing fire, and they lived in harmony with people and other creatures in all the islands of the Inland Sea. They were loved, revered, and considered to be special carriers of good luck for humans.

In those happy days, dragons were the favorite playmates of children, who loved to mount them, and go for long and exciting rides over the hills and waves, and through the sky. Forget-Me-Not's dragon-mother would sigh as she recalled the way she and the other dragons would spread their great scarlet-feathered wings to catch the currents of the wind, play hide-and-seek through high mounds of shining white clouds, and catch-me-if-you-can in and out of rainbow arches. Then her eyes would grow dark with sorrow, and her breath hot with anger as she told of the coming of a race of men who wielded cruel swords, and hated the playful power of dragons. The men drove them out of the islands wherever they could, banishing them to deserted places and dark caves. The children cried and begged for their lost playmates, but to no avail.

In the lonely, dark places of their banishment, the dragons developed sharp iron claws to protect themselves against the men who hunted them. They grew green scales to cover their vulnerable red bodies, and make them invisible among the green grasses and bushes that covered their lonely island homes. Sometimes, one of the dragons would begin smoldering with anger at the cruelty of the men who had made her suffer so. Then, in the night, she would spread her wings and soar low over villages where men lived, scorching their crops and burning their barns with her breath of flame. And while she was at it, she would raid their treasure houses and carry away their gold, silver, and jewels.

This is what Forget-Me-Not's mother had also done. Forget-Me-Not sometimes did the same. Although she had a considerate side, and was gentle with the plants and little creatures that lived on her island, she was fearsome when her anger flared. Then she would soar over the sea by night on great black bat-like wings to the places where the cruel, sword-wielding men lived. She was quick and clever, able to seize a great deal of treasure from the men while she struck terror into their hearts with her fiery breath and iron claws. Mind you, Forget-Me-Not never killed any of the men. She had her principles! But she did make life miserable for them. In return, they hated and hunted her. But so far, no one had been able to find her.

Year in and year out, Forget-Me-Not sat in her cave, with brilliant, icy-cold jewels and hard, shiny pieces of silver and gold scattered about her. They were cold comfort, and no company at all. And oh, how she longed for company. "If only a child would find its way here," she sighed to herself as she lay in the cave, or wandered about the island, looking for the special kind of rocks dragons like to eat.

Then, one bright day, her wish was granted. Forget-Me-Not was startled from a sound sleep by the sound of crying. Her eyes flew open. She poked her huge dragonhead out of the cave entrance. There, only a few feet from the cave was a teenage girl tied to a tree! The girl rubbed the tears from her eyes and looked about when she heard the sound of something moving near her. At the sight of the dragon, she began screaming non-stop. Forget-Me-Not waited patiently until the girl was too hoarse to scream any more, and slumped silent, pale, and trembling against the tree trunk.

"Please don't be afraid," said the dragon to the girl. "I won't hurt you, I promise. Tell me, how did you come to this island, and who tied you up to the tree?"

"I-I was brought here in a boat by one of the king's men," replied the girl in a surprised voice as she eyed the dragon warily.

"Why? asked the dragon gently.

"Because I wouldn't marry any one," replied the girl. "So my king-father banished me. His servants tied me to this tree and left me here." She began to cry.

"Oh dear, please don't cry," said the dragon. "It upsets me so! Here, I'll untie you and set you free. That'll make you feel better, won't it?" The girls shrank against the tree trunk as the dragon reached out with her razor sharp claws and ever so carefully cut the ropes around the girl's hands, feet, and waist without leaving the slightest scratch. As the last rope fell to the ground, the girls sank onto the long green grass next to the dragon, and fainted dead away. Forget-Me-Not didn't know what else to do except blow a little smoke in the girl's face, hoping it would help.

After awhile, the girl began choking and coughing, and sat up.

"Won't you tell me about yourself?" asked Forget-Me-Not as she laid her head next to the girl's feet.

With many cautious glances at the dragon, the girl told how her king—father had tried to make her marry a man who didn't love her. "He just bossed me around and treated me like a servant, and said mean things to me," she said with a toss of her head. "My friends had husbands who did the same thing to them. I decided I wasn't going to get married. It made my family really mad, especially my king-father, but I wouldn't give in to them." She scowled defiantly.

"I'm glad you didn't give in," replied Forget-Me-Not with a dragonish smile. "I've been wanting a playmate for ever so long. My mother told me all about you humans. I know what kind of food you like to eat, and where to find it on this island. You can share my cave with me, and I will protect you. We can go for rides and . . . ."

"O my!" interrupted the girl with a delighted gasp, " you remind me of the dragons my grandmother used to tell stories about. She says people and dragons got along famously until the men with the swords came to the islands of the Inner Sea. I thought they were just stories."

"They are true stories," retorted the dragon.

"But in the stories, dragons were bright red, with big feathered scarlet wings. They didn't have sharp claws, and they were happy and bringers of good luck," objected the girl.

"We were once that way," replied Forget-Me-Not sadly. "But we dragons have changed through the years since were attacked and driven away by the men with the swords."

"That's too bad!" exclaimed the girl. "You look miserable the way you are now. Oh, excuse me—I didn't mean to hurt your feelings."

"Well, you are right," returned the dragon. "I am miserable, and I'm sure I look it. I've been angry and sad and lonely for many, many years. You can't imagine how badly I have wanted someone to play with! You're a little older than what I had in mind, but at least you're a girl, so I don't have to worry about you growing into a sword-wielding cruel man."

The girl smiled at these words. She put out her hand and gently touched the dragon's cheek. "I'd be happy to keep you company," she said. "I want to learn all the things you can teach me, and play some of the games I heard about in the stories. Oh, it will be great fun!"

At this, Forget-Me-Not looked a great deal less miserable. And in the days and months that followed, she and the girl became fast friends. They wiled away countless happy hours wandering around the island, gathering food, telling stories, playing games with the treasure in the cave, and best of all, going for thrilling rides through clouds and over rainbows. The dragon became so happy, she stopped breathing fire and no longer went on angry raids to neighboring islands where her enemies lived. For her part, the girl was delighted to be free to do as she pleased for the first time in her life. In the dragon's company, she grew stronger and wiser and braver.

After awhile, however, she began to yearn for human company. The dragon could tell, and she worried about who might come, and what might happen then. Forget-Me-Not knew that when someone yearns with all their heart for something, it often happens. And she was right.

One fine day, human company arrived in the form of a young man whose name was George. He came riding from his blue-sailed ship anchored in the bay, spurring his white horse over the green hills. He wore a sword at his side, and a determined look on his face. He was searching every island of the Inland Sea for the king's daughter. The king had started to miss her, and regretted his hasty decision to banish her. He told his knights that whoever found her could marry her. He still thought of his daughter as his possession, and he wanted to see her again, because he loved her, in his own limited way. George was determined he would be the one to find the king's daughter. After all, a princess was a good catch, and would make his future as the king's son-in-law a bright one indeed.

After riding for a time around the edge of the island, and finding nothing, George struck out for the high hills at the center of the island so he could get a good view of the lay of the land. When he finally arrived at the top of the highest hill, panting and sweating, he saw, just below him in a little valley, a huge dragon! Next to it was the small, lithe form of a girl. Of course, he thought she was in terrible trouble, and would be devoured by the dragon. Down the hill he charged on his horse, brave as could be, his sword in hand, ready to attack the dragon and rescue the girl.

But Forget-Me-Not heard him coming, and rose to meet him. At the sight of his outstretched sword, her long-dormant anger flared up. Huge flames shot out of her mouth as she roared a warning. Spreading her wings over her friend, she extended her iron claws, and sent the sword clattering from George's hand as he came within her reach.

"Stop!" cried the dragon. "You don't know what you are doing!"

"Release the girl, you foul fiend!" replied George, and charged at the dragon again, though he was weaponless.

"You are a brave but foolish man!" exclaimed the dragon with eyes blazing furiously. "Will you just listen to us, for heaven's sake, before you come to grief."

"Us? Us? What do you mean, "us?" asked George in surprise as he brought his white horse to a sudden halt.

"That would be the girl and me," answered the dragon impatiently. "We are friends. It is her father the king she needs rescuing from, not me."

"This is the king's daughter?" cried George in surprise.

"Yes," answered the dragon.

"He promised me his daughter's hand in marriage if I could find her," said George as he looked at the girl out of the corner of his eye and noticed how lovely she was.

The girl stepped out from the shadows of the dragon's protective wings and faced George. "I am Princess Bluebell," she said, "and you may have found me, but my hand is not my father's to give. It belongs to me, and I will only give myself in love to one I freely and gladly choose, when and if I am ready!" Her eyes flashed and her voice was clear and strong as she spoke.

George gazed at her in speechless surprise. When he finally found words, he said, "Are you telling me that this dragon did not capture you and hold you prisoner?"

"That's right," said Princess Bluebell. "In fact, she freed me. It was my king-father who banished me to this deserted island because I wouldn't get married."

"Why wouldn't you want to get married?" asked George with a puzzled look on his face.

"Because I saw that the men who married my friends and sisters treated them like servants instead of friends and equals," replied Bluebell. "The man my father wanted me to marry treated me that way too."

"And it is men with swords like yours who drove me and my kind far from your shores, hunting and attacking us because you envied our power. That is why we are the miserable, iron-clawed, hard-scaled, fire-breathing creatures we are now," added the dragon in an angry voice. "Do you wonder that we seize your treasure and terrorize you in the night?"

George had nothing to say, but he looked again at Princess Bluebell, who cried, "If it weren't for the dragon and our friendship, I wouldn't be alive today!"

"Then I was told a lie!" exclaimed George as his face turned red. "The king said you were captured and carried away by the dragon. But if what you are both saying is true, then the old stories of happy red dragons playing with children and living in harmony with people are more than old wives' tales."

"Old wives' tales are often true stories some people would rather not believe," retorted Forget-Me-Not.

George couldn't find another thing to say. He sat down suddenly on the ground as if it was all too much for him. He stayed silent, and began to think many new thoughts. Forget-Me-Not and Bluebell left him alone except to bring him food and drink. This went on for several days. At night, the dragon lit a fire with her breath to help keep George warm in the cold night air. She could tell he was changing inside, and that it was for the good.

One morning, as the sky turned pale blue and pink with the coming of dawn, George, who was alone at the time, leaped to his feet, seized his sword, which was still lying nearby, and went looking for Princess Bluebell.

When he finally found her walking in the woods, he fell on his knees before her and said, "Please, please forgive me and my foolish fellow men for not treating you and your sisters and friends with love and respect. I ask your permission to live here on the island and learn from you and the dragon. I offer you my sword as a sign of my willingness to change, to honor you and other girls and women, and teach my fellow men to do the same."

At these words, Princess Bluebell smiled into George's earnest face, kissed him lightly on the forehead, and raised him to his feet. Taking the sword in her hand, she thrust it deep into the earth up to its hilt. "Let it stay here, and let the grasses and vines cover it," she said. Then, taking his hand, she led George to the cave where the dragon was napping. Forget-Me-Not heard them coming, and met them at the entrance.

"May George stay here for awhile and learn to be our friend?" asked Princess Bluebell. The dragon noticed he no longer had his sword. She looked long and deep into George's clear eyes, and solemnly nodded. George and Princess Bluebell smiled and hugged each other as Forget-Me-Not spread her huge wings over them.

In the days and months that followed, a strange and wonderful thing happened. The dragon gradually began to shed her hard green scales. Her claws shrank to almost nothing. Her skin grew smooth and red. Her wings grew soft scarlet feathers. Her breath became sweet and cool as a spring breeze blowing through lilies. And all the while, the friendship between George and Princess Bluebell grew and grew, until the day she gladly and freely gave her hand to him, and they were united in a deep and true love.

On that glad day, the dragon gave George and Princess Bluebell all the treasure she had been guarding in her cave. "I have no use for it," she said as she laid the flashing jewels and gleaming gold and silver at their feet. "But you will have need of it in time to come. For it is your destiny to rule the islands of the Inland Sea in place of the present king, and restore the old harmony between dragons and humans, and between men and women. The treasures you will need for your reign in these islands are here before you. Use them well. And good luck!"

With these words, Forget-Me-Not stretched out her huge, scarlet-feathered wings in blessing and soared, laughing, into the sunrise.

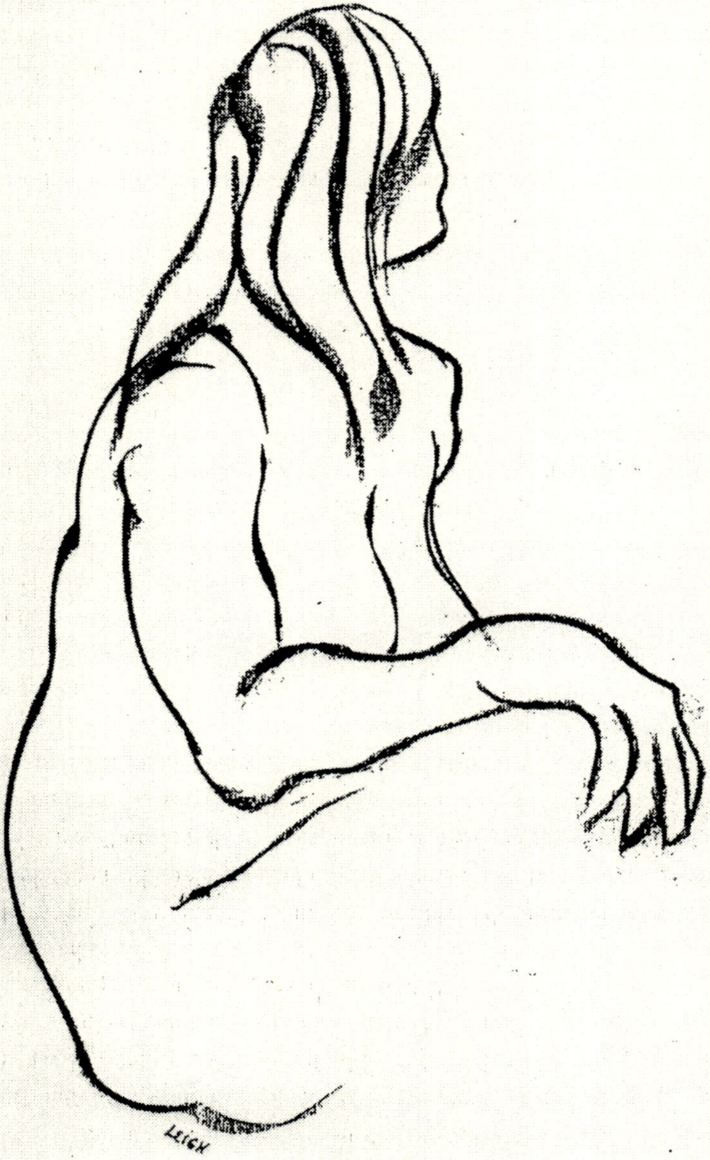
LEIGH

CHAPTER EIGHT

THE POWER OF OUR MYTHS

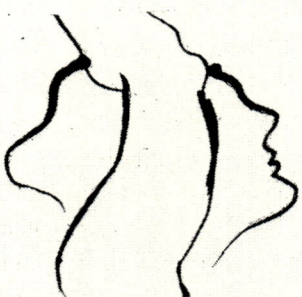

There are myths that have come down to us through the ages, and there are myths that we are creating in our own lifetimes. The myths of previous ages reflect the soul-deep beliefs and patterns of life from past cultures. The stories they tell reveal the particular ways in which men and women of old related to each other and to the situations in which they found themselves. These myths contain the wisdom and folly of our human ancestors. Insofar as they continue to resonate with our lives, they continue to have power for us.

Joseph Campbell, whose writings on mythology have had such great impact on people now living, says that myths are archetypal stories that both reflect and shape human life. Archetypes are powerful patterns of belief and behavior that are rooted in the collective unconscious of the human race. They are to humans what instincts are to animals. We believe and act in certain "instinctive" patterns, or Archetypes. We play the fool, go on heroic quests and journeys, learn wisdom from a Wise Old Man or Woman, wait for Prince Charming to rescue us, slay the Dragon, find a lost treasure, get lost in deep woods, and so on.

We can recognize these Archetypes in our dreams, legends, myths, and fairy tales, and even in our outer lives in some form. It is a good thing to be aware of them and how they are shaping our lives, so that we can consciously choose which ones we find helpful, and free ourselves from the influence of those which are not. For instance, women today may not find it helpful to live out the Archetype of Cinderella or Sleeping Beauty by passively waiting for a man to rescue them from an unsatisfactory life. They might also find it more helpful to consult Wise Old Woman wisdom than Wise Old Man wisdom, given all that we have been talking about in this book!

In India, for instance, the wisdom of ancient male sages is revealed in the myth of Ram and Sita. Unfortunately, it is, among other things, a story that continues to reinforce the Archetype of the dutiful, beautiful, submissive, and utterly devoted wife whose husband is a virtual god in her life. I recently asked a young Indian woman about the influence of this myth on her generation. She said "We are saying that if a man is as god-like as Ram, we might consider being a wife like Sita to him. Of course, there are no such men! So if they can't be like Ram, why should we try to be like Sita?"

When I look at myths we have inherited from the past, I can see layers of meaning in them. The deepest layer tells, in symbolic language, what has been and perhaps still is going on in the human soul. It is like a vivid collective dream. Another layer reveals the underlying beliefs of the culture that shaped the myth. Still another layer reveals the outer social situation of men and women in a certain time and place. The danger is in regarding myths as if they were depictions of "what was, is now, and ever shall be, world without end." When we regard them in this way, we are "under their spell," so to speak. Then they reinforce age-old stereotypes about women and men and their relationships that continue to live in our psyche, out of our awareness. When we are under a spell, we are not free to be who we really are, as all the old myths teach us.

We need to break the spell of these old myths. They need to be seen, not as determining our lives, but as revealing the hidden beliefs, assumptions, and patterns of life in our collective past. To realize they are not "set in stone," is to break their hold on our souls and allow us to choose more freely what we believe and how we will live. Modern myths, like *Star Wars* and the *Lord of the Rings*, still largely reflect the old Archetypes about men and women, good and evil, and the "myth of redemptive violence." This is Walter Wink's term, used in his book *The Powers-That-Be*, to describe the nearly universal belief that the only way to defeat evil is violently.

However, some myths of our time do reflect changes in the collective unconscious about the role and potential of women. The movie "Schreck", which is a playful modern fairy story with many allusions to traditional western fairy tales, is a good illustration of a very different depiction of males and females and their relationship to each other. With wonderful wit and humor, it pictures a new view of women and men that is taking hold in modern culture.

This is happening because more and more people are choosing different beliefs and living lives in different patterns than those pictured in the myths of the past. New Archetypes are being born in the collective unconscious that support the emergence of true partnership between women and men, and a flourishing world.

These new Archetypes are coming into our consciousness through certain artists, and in dreams, visions, and processes like Active Imagination. (This process is described in Carl Jung's books.) Together, they are producing new myths for evolving humanity.

Each one of us, because we are a part of the whole, can be a channel through which these new myths come into consciousness. Robert Johnson, in his fine book *Inner Work*, talks about the process of Active Imagination, and how anyone can do it. He tells of people he has counseled who have created a powerful new personal myth for themselves in this way. Because we are all connected at a deep soul level, these personal myths also have a universal dimension. It is a wonderful experience to discover your own personal myth. It reveals the pattern, purpose, and meaning of your life, your soul's "code." You might want to try Active Imagination to see what emerges as your myth.

I have personally tried this method, and found it works well for me. I would like to share one of the personal myths that was born into my consciousness via the Active Imagination process. I believe it reveals not only deep soul patterns in my own life, but also Archetypes that are developing in the collective unconscious as the human race goes through this time of huge crisis and transition. You will notice right away that there is an obvious relationship between this mythical story and N.E.W., although the story came to me before the idea for N.E.W. surfaced in my consciousness. This is because our personal myths often portray our future more than our past, and serve as a guiding pattern as we go forward into the rest of our life.

I share this personal myth with you in the hope that it will evoke *your* myths, so that you can experience first hand their power to inspire your life with purpose and meaning, and reveal its underlying spiritual pattern. The myth I share here has been an important source of the courage and conviction I needed to persevere in my life task of empowering women. It is because I believe it also reveals what is happening at a deep soul level in the collective unconscious that I have hope for the future. (Of course, I have other reasons for hoping too, including my strong belief in Amazing Grace!)

Because myths come clothed in vivid, compelling images that capture our hearts and imaginations, they have a great deal of power to shape our reality. When we *deliberately choose* to live out the life-giving beliefs and values of our own myths, we are empowered by their vital energies, and guided by their deep wisdom to be true to our best, most powerful selves. That has been my experience, and I hope it will be yours as well as you read this personal myth, and ponder how it speaks to you.

THE AMAZONS AND THE DRAGON

I am floating in a long dugout canoe on the Amazon River as it winds through deep jungle. It is night, and the jungle is vibrating with the deep beat of a great Drum somewhere in its depths. I am carrying a torch to light the way and protect me. I hear many creature noises as I glide along, carried by the Amazon's mighty current. A half moon shines high above, coating the river with silver light. Great cat eyes shine from the darkness on both sides. I look into their eyes as I pass by, and I feel them looking into mine. I sense us exchanging energies, and my body begins to feel like a great cat's body—lithe, strong, alert, ready for whatever comes.

Suddenly, I hear a roar, and one of the pairs of eyes moves towards me with the swiftness of lightening. It is a huge Black Jaguar. She swims alongside the canoe, her dark head gleaming in the torchlight. Words that are not mine form in my mind as I watch her. "I am here to guide and protect you. Don't be afraid."

I try to let go of my fear and relax as I float on and on with the river's flow until the moon sinks behind the trees ahead, and the sky starts to turn pearl gray with the coming of dawn. All at once, the Black Jaguar takes a flying leap, and lands on the bank on my right. She lopes along, staying even with my canoe until the river curves and the current carries my canoe on to a narrow spit of sand.

I climb out, and lift my torch high to greet the rising sun in the east. Then I dowse it in the water and put it down in the canoe. Again, words form in my mind out of nowhere. "Keep the torch with you. You may need it." I know at once it is the Black Jaguar communing with me again. "I wonder how she does that?" I ask as I pick up the torch. In reply I hear the words, "I am kything with you. I fix your image strongly in my mind, merge with it, and create the words I want you to hear. You can do this with me as well. " She turns into the jungle, heading east. "Follow me," she kythes.

As I walk behind her, the light of dawn gleams on the huge leaves and vines through which we make our way. Brilliantly colored flowers of kinds I have never seen blossom everywhere. Birds whose feathers rival the rainbow colors of the flowers flash through the canopy above, singing their morning songs. Eventually, we come to a swampy place, and the Black Jaguar tells me to ride on her back for a while. The velvet feel of her black fur, and the rippling of her great muscles beneath my bare legs convey a sensual strength I have never felt before. I am aware of how much I enjoy it as we go ever deeper into the jungle.

Presently, we come to a pile of marble ruins covered with vines. "What are these?" I kythe as the Black Jaguar stops. She sits down, and I dismount and sit next to her facing the ruins.

"This was a place of captivity," she growls. "Wild ones like us were caught, trapped, locked up here in cages, and made to serve the selfish and vain purposes of the men who fancied themselves rulers over the animal kingdom as well as their own."

"What happened?" I ask as I gaze around, noticing how the jungle has reclaimed its ground and over-run the buildings.

"They over-reached. They tried to conquer and control the Amazons. They were overcome in the end."

"Who are the Amazons?" I ask. "Do they live anywhere near here?"

"Oh yes, but deeper in and further up, on the slopes of the Mountains of the Moon," replies my Black Jaguar guide.

"Is it possible for me to meet them?" I ask impulsively. She looks at me with a penetrating gaze. "Yes. But you may find the meeting uncomfortable."

"Why?"

"Their fierceness is not easy to face. These are not tame women."

"Like me?"

"Like you. Yet I know there is a wild woman in you too, or you would not even consider asking to meet an Amazon!"

"Perhaps, if I meet one, she can help free the one in me," I reply, with a little shiver of fear, and a tingle of excitement at the same time.

"You must be ready for such freedom," kythes the Black Jaguar, looking again into my eyes in a way that sees right through me. "There are tests you must pass first. If this is truly what your heart desires, go yonder by that huge mahogany tree, lean against it, shut your eyes, and watch what images come. To help you, I suggest you call Sybil, the Great Python. She will know what to do for you."

I swallow hard. But something drives me to continue. "How do I call her?" I ask.

"You must imagine what it feels like to be a python. Begin to move like one, and make sounds that feel like snake language. Forget about yourself and how you look or feel. Just focus on her with your whole being."

"Easier said than done," I mutter to myself. I recall the times I have seen pythons in zoos, and how they move. I have no idea how they sound, but I have to trust that the right ones will come to mind as I begin moving in a snake dance. I am amazed at how quickly the feeling of actually being a snake takes over, and soon lots of hissing sounds are coming from my mouth. I can feel my body undulating gracefully as I move in a circle. I begin to actually enjoy the feeling.

At that moment, I see a huge python emerging from under the roots of the mahogany tree! She uncoils her enormous length, and slithers into a spiral around me. I stand in the middle of her coils. She raises her head to face me.

"I need your help, " I kythe, "though how, I don't yet know. Your friend Black Jaguar tells me I am to sit at the base of the mahogany tree and see what images come to me."

" I will curl up opposite you," kythes Sybil. "As the images come, speak them out loud, and I will know what to do to help you."

"Good!" I exclaim, with a strange sense of relief. "Black Jaguar, will you sit on my left by the tree, and let me rest my hand on your back as I sit there? And by the way, what is your name? May I use it?"

"Yes. My name is Kalee. And I will sit next to you to support you through this test. Anything I can do to help free the wild woman in you . . ."

I lean back against the great Mahogany Tree, and allow myself to feel its supporting energy. I close my eyes, and imagine the White Light of Great Spirit filling my body and shining in a protective circle of light around me. I breathe deeply, in through my nose, out through my mouth, and silently wait.

The first image that comes to me is of a huge white-skinned Amazon woman, dressed in a leopard skin like a short tunic, with flowing golden hair. She has a gold sword in one hand, and a gold shield studded with diamonds in the other. Her sapphire blue eyes are blazing with anger. Her skin is scarred from many battles. As her eyes meet mine, I turn ice-cold. I remember the presence of Sybil, and I manage to stammer out loud what I am seeing. Somehow, this makes me feel better. Just knowing Sybil is opposite me, listening and watching, lessens my fear.

Next comes a huge red-haired Amazon whose hair flies out like flames from her head. She carries flame—throwers, and her green eyes blaze with fury. Her body is covered with a copper chain-link suit of armor. As her eyes meet mine, I feel as if I am burning up. Again, I get a grip on myself and manage to describe her appearance aloud for Sybil. As soon as I finish, I see a huge, brown-skinned Amazon with long disheveled black hair, and brown eyes dark with rage. She is holding a mace and dagger in her two hands. She is wearing a blood red tunic and pants. When her eyes meet mine, I start to shiver. I describe her aloud to Sybil, and feel a wave of relief. Along comes the next Amazon—a huge black-skinned woman with long dreadlocks, and armed with a spear in each hand. She is wearing a many layered necklace of elephants carved from ivory which covers her torso, and an apron of bright colored beads which she wears like a short skirt. When her angry gaze meets mine, I feel a strong stab in my heart. I gasp out what I see for Sybil, and take several deep breaths to calm myself. Last comes a huge golden-skinned Amazon with wild, short straight black hair that sticks out like a crown of spikes from her head. Her black eyes flash fiercely, and in her hands she carries grenades. When our eyes meet, I feel caught up in a whirlwind of energy that takes my breath away. I feel as if I will pass out. The energy of the Amazon Women's combined rage and power is overwhelming, even when I describe them aloud for Sybil.

"Open your eyes," kythes the Python. I do, and find myself looking into her calm, detached gaze. "Just keep observing, as if you were going to paint them," hisses Sybil. "Don't let their energy swallow you up."

I close my eyes again, and see the five huge Amazon Women join hands, and circle the tree and me. A Drumbeat that shakes my bones begins, and the forest quivers to its sound. The Amazons begins to dance with the beat, which becomes ever faster and more furious. I grow dizzy watching. Then, just as suddenly, the Drum beat stops, and the Amazons line up facing me, sweating, panting, and awesome in their raw power. I imagine painting them standing there in all their glory. This strengthens the observer part of me, and I feel able to relate to them.

"Who are you?" I ask.

"The repressed power and rage of all women through untold centuries," they reply with one voice.

"Why have you come to me?" I ask.

"You wanted us to come to you, did you not?" they reply.

"Yes, I did. I didn't realize how incredibly powerful and awe-full you are," I reply with a little shudder.

"Are you afraid of us?" they ask.

I pause to ponder the question. I want to answer it as honestly as I can. "I am afraid, but I sense no desire on your part to hurt me," I respond. "Still, if you were ever let loose in the world . . ."

"What then?" they ask.

"I wish I knew," I reply.

In a flash, right in front of me, I see a vision of five spirals, each made up of millions of women from all over the world. At the center of each spiral stands one of the Amazons. I hear them shouting out to the spirals of women in a loud voice,

> *"Why do you continue to allow the rape of the earth, yourselves, and your children?*
> *Why do you not claim your ancient power as women, and rise up to take your place as givers and shapers of life?*
> *Do you see these weapons we carry?*
> *They need to be taken out of the hands of men, and transformed by you into instruments of peace.*
> *You have the power to do this. Stop holding yourselves back.*
> *Your fear of men must be overcome.*
> *If they continue in their ways, everyone and everything in the world will perish.*
> *Do not believe their lies about your nature and place.*
> *Do not assent to the way they have arranged your lives.*
> *Women of the world, unite!*
> *BE who you really are! We are the image of your power.*
> *Use it or lose it!"*

The Drum begins again. As its beat gets louder and stronger, I see the women in the five spirals take each other's hands and begin dancing and chanting.

> *"The Day has come to end the ancient wrong.*
> *Our weapon is Divine Love. Our hearts are strong.*
> *Nothing and no one can stop us. The tide has turned.*
> *Now we will put to use the lessons we've learned.*
> *Gone will be those who dominate and destroy.*
> *Women and men will support all of life with joy.*
> *We will not give up. We will not give in.*
> *We will live as full partners with men.*
> *We will abolish greed and strife.*
> *We will birth a world of flourishing life.*

The spirals of women, millions and millions of them, are alive with ever expanding energy fueled by outrage, determination, love, and courage. It radiates out in huge waves of power that keep growing.

Then the vision fades. I find myself face to face with the five Amazons. "If only this vision could come true soon!" I cry.

"Will you let us loose on the world?" they reply.

"Yes! Yes! Yes!" I exclaim. "With your energy freed in them, the women of the world can do what the vision showed. I am sure of it."

The five Amazons smile radiantly, and I realize there is far more to them than their anger. Once again, they make a circle, and invite me into its Center. A hidden Drum in the jungle sounds the heart beat of Mother Earth. They begin to dance, and as they do, I feel their huge energy pouring into me, empowering me to empower women. I feel myself a part of their dance of power, and the dance goes on and on.

Finally, the Drumbeat fades away, as do the Amazons, and I am in the jungle alone with only Kalee at my side.

"You have passed the test," she says. "You met the Amazons through images in your mind. You stood your ground and faced your fears. You opened up to their energy, and took it into yourself. That wild woman in you is finally free enough to join the Amazons in the battle to defeat the Dragon of Domination once and for all. The time is finally ripe. And so are you."

"You mean—this was just a warm up exercise for the Real Thing?" I gasp. I can feel my heart beating faster. Kalee nods, and tells me to get on her back again. Once more, a great Drum beats in the heart of the Jungle. Kalee takes me towards the place where the Drum seems to be beating. I look up at the moon shining high above us, lighting our way.

All at once, I become aware of huge black shadows coming towards us. As we draw nearer to them, and they to us, I can see that they are Amazons, each one riding a great cat. A Chinese looking Amazon is riding a Siberian tiger. An Indian looking Amazon is riding a Bengal tiger. An African looking Amazon is riding a black-maned lion. A European looking Amazon is riding a mountain lion. A Native American looking Amazon is riding on a spotted jaguar. There are more, but I cannot make them out in the dark shadows. Together, we ride silently towards the Drumbeat.

Eventually, we emerge into a big circular clearing in the jungle. At its center is a large fire, its flames leaping up towards the stars. A white-haired Native American woman is playing a great Mother Drum near the fire. Its light flickers on her ancient face as we gather in a circle around the leaping flames. I look up, and see flying above us, silhouetted against the moon, a huge snowy owl. "That is Athena," kythes Kalee. "She will be a part of our expedition. So will Sybil. See! She lies coiled at Grand Mother's feet."

The Drum falls silent. A hush falls over the jungle. Athena flies down and alights on Grand Mother's head. "Are you all ready?" asks Grand Mother solemnly. "This will be the fight of your life against the Ancient Dragon of Domination. Its greed and destructiveness knows no bounds. It will do anything to survive. The usual weapons will not prevail against this monstrous Dragon. Its hide is so thick nothing can penetrate it. "

"Grand Mother," I cry. "Has it no soft spot? No vulnerable place? No spark of Holy Fire?"

"It does," says Grand Mother with a smile. "But the weapons of your rage cannot hurt it. The Dragon has power because it too has a spark of Divine Life at its core. Only if that core is penetrated, and the Divine Spark released, will you prevail."

"But Grand Mother, how are we to do that?" I ask with a sinking feeling in the pit of my stomach.

"You must all enter into the Great Silence within and listen for Divine Wisdom. You will be guided if you open your hearts with trust."

The Amazons look at Grand Mother, each other, and me. As one, we dismount from our great cats, and sit next to them, facing the fire. A deep silence surrounds us as we sit listening to the wisdom deep within our souls. Our big cat companions begin purring softly, as if to encourage us with the vibrations of their magnificent bodies next to ours.

After awhile, we begin to speak out loud the guidance we are receiving.

"Encircle the Dragon all at once, and from every perspective in the circle shout out your truth boldly."

"The Dragon will be furious and lash out at you. When it comes at you, withdraw, while those positioned behind it advance, shouting fearlessly."

"Light the torches I have for you from my Sacred Heart Fire here at the Center. Let your torches blaze as you proclaim your truth. Get as near as you can to the Dragon, and hold your fire to its hide. The heat will cause its scales to burn, and make it harder for it to attack you."

"Above all, do not fear, and trust that if you do all this, you will overcome the Beast. You will know in the moment what to do next, and the help you need will come to you. Go! Act! Now!"

As we finish sharing our Divine Guidance, I look around the circle of Amazons. How hugely powerful and beautiful they are. They represent women everywhere, and my heart swells with love and pride and gratitude. One by one, they step forward to receive a blazing torch from Grand Mother. I hold out the torch I took with me into the jungle from my canoe, and she lights it as she looks deeply into my soul through my eyes. I feel her healing love penetrate every fiber of my being, and I know, deep down, that no matter what happens, all will be well.

"Nothing can put this fire out!" she says to us. "Aim your flame of truth well as you fight for the right." Then she sounds the great Drum of Mother Earth's Heart Beat, and it fills us with courage for the battle ahead. Silently, we move single file into the jungle, riding our big cats. "Sybil knows where the Dragon dwells, and will lead you to it," calls Grand Mother.

We follow the Great Python, our torches lighting the way as we snake through the dark jungle. Athena flies overhead, watching everything. After many hours, we finally enter a huge, scorched clearing. At its center is a big black hole, with foul smelling smoke coming out of it. The hiss of Dragon breath can be heard emerging from the hole as we get closer to it. The Dragon seems to be sensing that something is amiss. We can hear it moving in the darkness below. The big cats growl and howl as its fearsome head emerges. "Now!" screeches Athena from overhead. "Attack with your torches of truth!"

As the Dragon crawls out of the darkness into the light of our torches, its green eyes gleam with malice. The putrid smell of sulfur fills the air around us. Athena hovers above us, fanning her great wings to help dispel the stink. The Dragon's body keeps coming out of the hole—dark, slimy, scaled, clawed, gigantic. It opens its mouth and roars. The sound shakes the dead trees around the clearing, and makes our ears ache. Its teeth gleam like javelins in the firelight.

In spite of our fear, we begin shouting our truth as loudly as we can awhile we thrust our burning torches at the Dragon.

"Your time for ruining the life of this earth is up."

"Your power relies on force and fear. It is weak at the core. It is nothing compared with our life-giving power."

"We no longer believe your lies. Things can and will change."

"We will not fear your threats or endure your destructive ways."

Then all together, with the big cats backing us up, we roar over and over again, "Enough is enough! You must give up!"

At these words, the Dragon grows visibly angrier. But it controls its rage and with a sneer says, "Puny women! You imagine you can undo *my* power? I have always dominated the earth, and I always will. You are powerless against me!" It casts its hypnotic evil stare on the Amazons facing it, and lashes out at them with one of its cruel claws. They withdraw, and the rest of us charge at the Dragon from behind, thrusting our torches into its massive body and tail.

At this, it roars with pain and rage, and whirling around, lunges at us bellowing, "I have destroyed you witches and bitches before, and I will do it again. Flee back to your proper place or die!"

Our big cats are quick enough to dodge its lunges, and we all take turns shouting our truths and thrusting our torches into its hide. The Dragon is beside itself with rage, lunging this way and that, but never able to reach anyone with its blows. This goes on and on for hours. Each time we feel weary, Athena cries from above, "Never stop! Never give up!" We begin to sing loudly in unison, and then in glorious harmony, "We shall overcome."

To our surprise, we notice that our singing seems to dismay the Dragon. It falters for a moment and grows visibly weaker. Its lunges are shorter and further apart. We keep singing and singing, stinging its hide with our burning torches. Somehow, our energy does not give out. But we are relieved to see light finally creeping into the sky, heralding the coming of a New Day. We sense we are at a crisis point, and wonder what to do next. We don't want the Dragon to crawl back in its hole, for we know we have not yet prevailed, and it will just come out to fight another day. We have no idea how to reach that Divine spark of life at its core and release it. We all offer silent prayers for help from Great Spirit, and guidance for what to do next.

Suddenly, Athena lets out an ear splitting screech, as only an owl can, and swoops down at the Dragon. Startled, it raises its eyes to look at Athena. Like white lightening, she pierces its eyes with her talons and silently swoops back up into the sky, circling the Dragon. It roars with pain, blinded, unable to see in its old ways, black blood streaming down its face. As it opens its huge jaws in anguish, Sybil the snake crawls swiftly into its throat and disappears. We gasp in dismay. The Dragon writhes and turns over, thrashing its limbs and tail, exposing its soft, unprotected red underbelly.

At this moment, birds all around us burst into song, and the sun's first rays gleam on the treetops. We look up and behold a line of hummingbirds flying swiftly towards us from the brightness of the eastern sky. Looking like a long, iridescent spear, they dive into the Dragon's under belly, their long sharp beaks aimed at one central point. The Dragon shrieks and moans. Rose red blood pours from the place the humming birds are piercing through.

After a while, we notice that the Dragon's shrieks and moans are changing in tone from pain and anger to ecstasy, as if it were experiencing huge pleasure! We all begin laughing, even though this is puzzling indeed. The humming birds continue their piercing until the Dragon lies inert and exhausted. Then they perch on the branches of the bare, dragon-scorched trees at the edge of the clearing. To our amazement, the trees turn green with new life—budding, leafing, blossoming, and bearing fruit, right before our eyes, as if time has suddenly speeded up.

Out of the black hole near the Dragon, a steaming geyser of water gushes upward, and the drops of water at its summit shine with rainbow colors in the light of the rising sun. Out of the hole pierced by the hummingbirds in the Dragon's belly crawls Sybil. We all clap and cheer as the Great Python coils and uncoils herself free of the Dragon's body. To our added amazement, a bright spark of fire flies upward from the hole in the Dragon's belly into the blue sky above. It transforms into a Phoenix, and at that same moment, the body of the Dragon disappears in a puff of smoke, leaving a nest of ashes in its place. In the center of the ash nest is one huge, perfect Pearl.

As we stand gazing at the Pearl in disbelief, we hear the laughter of many children around us. Out of the jungle they run, singing, clapping, and dancing around us in a circle as they say, "Ding Dong, the Dragon's Dead!" Above us, I notice the Phoenix hovering for a long moment before it flies towards the rising sun, merging with it in a spectacular flash of light.

I motion for silence, and say, "Let's hear what happened to Sybil after she so bravely crawled right inside the Dragon." Everyone cheers their agreement, and Sybil clears her very long throat and begins.

"I felt this urge to get inside the Dragon as it was roaring after Athena attacked its eyes. I crawled down its throat into its dark, smelly belly. It's a good thing I can see in the dark, because there was a huge, barnacled oyster in there, clamped shut. I knew I had to pry that shell open, though I didn't know why. The only way I could do it, in the end, was to wrap my coils around it and tighten them until the shell cracked and buckled open. Out poured the most delicious rose fragrance, which somehow changed the filthy water inside the dragon's belly into golden honey! Inside the shell I saw a huge, perfect pearl glowing in the dark. Its radiance was so bright, it lit up the cavernous innards of the Dragon—all sharp and jagged and strewn with the undigested remains of whatever the Dragon swallowed. Ugh! I've never been in such an awful place. But the rose fragrance, the radiant pearl light, and the sweet amber flow of honey coating the cavity of the belly changed everything.

It was at this point that I felt the Dragon writhing and turning over on its back. After that, I could see the sharp, long beaks of the hummingbirds piercing the thin skin of its belly right above my head.

Before long, the hole was big enough for me to crawl out, and here I am! I'm glad *that's* over."

"What you did took a lot of courage and wisdom," I say to Sybil.

The python bows her head and says, "I had a lot of Divine help, or I couldn't have done it." With these words, she crawls to the nest of ashes, takes the gleaming Pearl from it, and brings it to me. I cup my hands to receive it with delight, amazement, and gratitude. I hold it out for all to see. "This is the Pearl of our true nature," I cry. "It belongs to us all. Hold out your hands to receive it, dear ones!"

The Amazons and the children hold out their left hands, and as they do, the Pearl appears in every one! "Let's treasure this wonderful Pearl in our hearts always, so that all of Life may flourish in joy and love everywhere," I say. We all clasp the Pearl to our hearts, and there It is, to this day.

* * *

Have you noticed that this myth is in the present tense? That is because it is not something that happened once, but is an ongoing reality. It is not really finished either. It remains open-ended. If you can identify with this mythical story, feel free to live into it with your imagination and become the "I" who is telling the story. Then, if you are drawn to do so, continue the story in your own way. Pretend it is your story too, and see what happens.

Of course, you are also encouraged to do what I did, and create your own, using the Active Imagination process described in the book *Inner Work* by Robert Johnson. It is an exciting soul adventure, open to anyone. If you want to share what you write, e-mail it to me, (marchiene@earthlink.net) and we will consider it for inclusion on the N.E.W. website. (*www.networktoempowerwomen.com*) In this way, we can empower each other with our stories, and even co-create grand new myths for our time which will empower women and men to fly through life together as true partners in Life and Love.

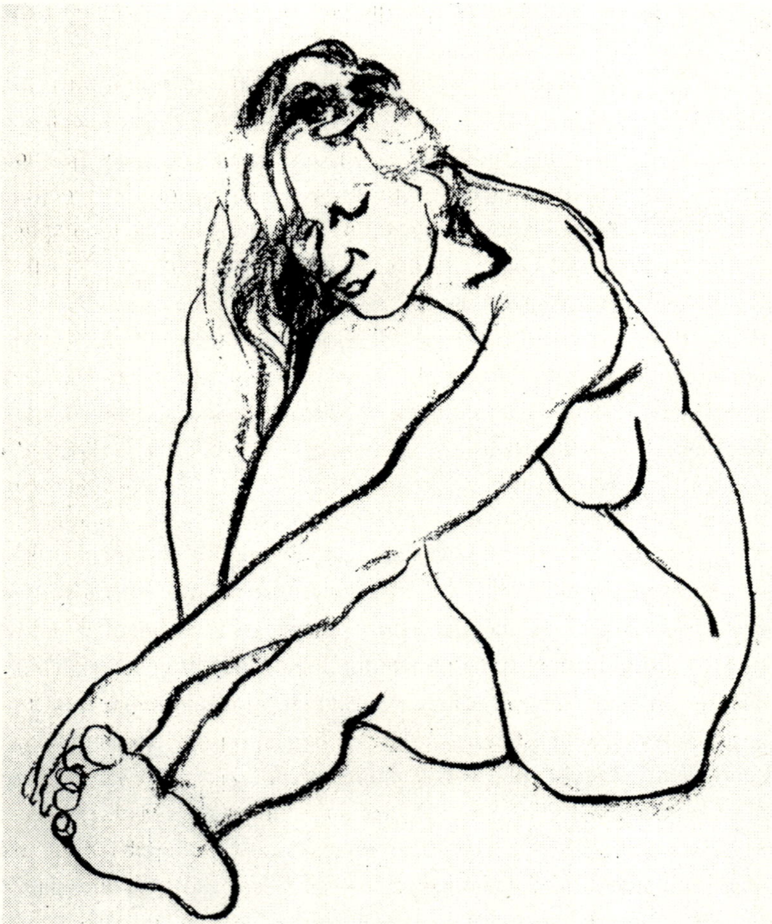
LEIGH

CHAPTER NINE

THE POWER OF YOUR CHOOSING

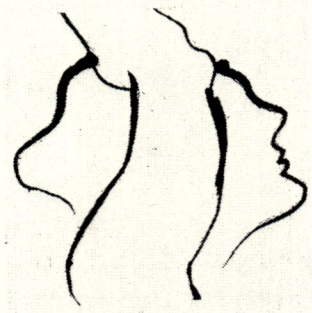

THE FUTURE FOR WOMEN - A N.E.W. BOOK

This chapter is yours to write. On these pages you can reflect, question, create your own stories, record insights and ideas, draw feelings, or anything else you choose. Just as the Ninth Question is your choice in the N.E.W. Circle Process, so also, this Ninth chapter is up to you to create. In this way, you can make The N.E.W. Book your own. If you have not already underlined, checked, starred, and otherwise noted your responses in the margins of this book's previous pages, please feel free to do so. Then use this chapter to expand your response. If there is something you would like to have read in this book, but found it wasn't there, write it here.

You are also invited to share your thoughts and feelings in the forum on the N.E.W. website: *www.networktoempowerwomen.com.*

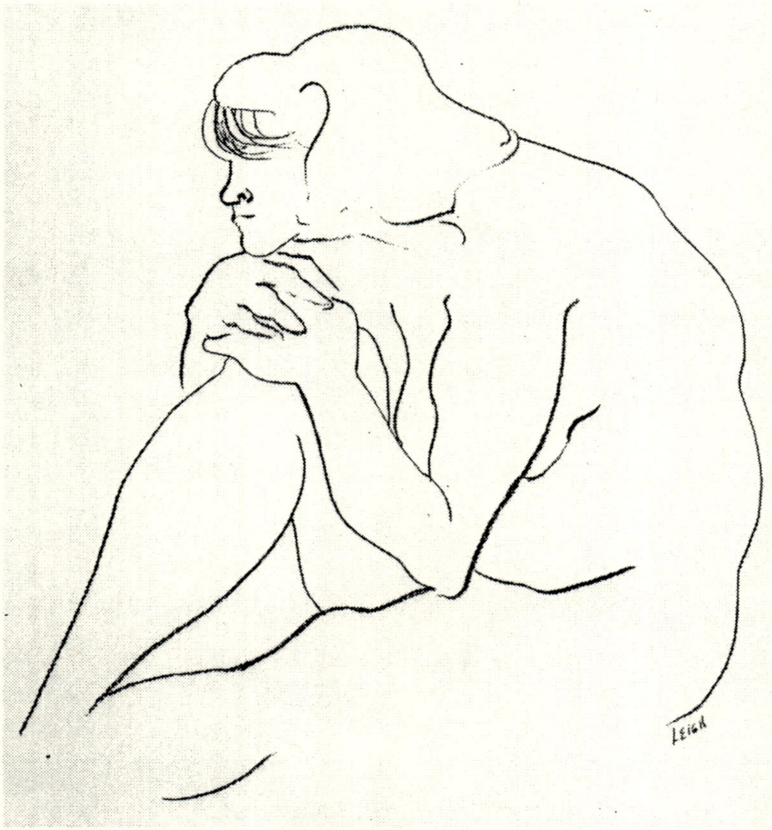
LEIGH

BIBLIOGRAPHY

Baldwin, Christina. *Calling the Circle: The First and Future Culture* (New York: Bantam Books, 1998).

Bolen, Jean Shinoda. *The Millionth Circle: How to Change Ourselves and the World* (Berkeley, CA: Conari Press, 1999).

Christ & Plaskow, ed. *Womanspirit Rising* (Harper SanFrancisco, 1992).

Duerk, Judith. *Circle of Stones: Woman's Journey to Herself* (San Diego, CA: LuraMedia, 1990).

Eisler, Riane. *The Chalice and the Blade: Our History, Our Future* (San Francisco: Harper & Rowe, 1987).

Gawain, Shakti. *The Path of Transformation* (Mill Valley, CA: Nataraj Publishing 1993).

Gimbutas, Marija. *The Language of the Goddess* (Harper SanFrancisco, 1991).

Grabhorn, Lynn. *Excuse Me, Your Life Is Waiting* (Hampton Roads Publishing, 2000).

Hagberg, Janet O. *Real Power* (Salem, WI: Sheffield Publishing Co., 2003).

Hay, Louise L. *Empowering Women* (Carlsbad, CA: Hay House, Inc. 1997)

Johnson, Allan G. *The Gender Knot: Unraveling Our Patriarchal Legacy* (Philadelphia: Temple University Press, 1997).

Katie, Byron. *Loving What Is* (New York: Harmony Books, 2002).

Lyons, Alana. *Now It's Our Turn: How Women Can Transform Their Lives and Save the Planet* (Malibu, CA: Jaguar Books, 1998).

Palmer, Harry. *Living Deliberately* (Star's Edge International, 1994).

Ryan, M.J., Ed. *The Fabric of the Future: Women Visionaries Illuminate the Path to Tomorrow* (Berkley, CA: Conari Press, 1998).

Schaef, Anne Wilson. *Women's Reality* (New York: Harper Collins, 1981).

Waya, Ai Gvhdi. *Path of the Mystic* (Sedona, AZ: Light Technology Publishing, 1997).

RESOURCE APPENDIX

This resource appendix is a listing of some of the many resources that already exist for the empowering of women. This is, in itself, a most encouraging state of affairs. The bibliography, and the bibliographies at the back of the books in it, could provide enough good reading for a year or more. There are so many books I could recommend, the listing of them would be overwhelming. Therefore, I am listing one category of books here which I have read, and judge to be of the greatest value. They are "must reads," if you will. The second category of books contains title I have read and that have been highly recommended to me by friends whose judgment I respect. There will be many more books listed on the N.E.W. website.

I am also including other websites that empower women. You, the reader, can find many, many more by searching for them on the World Wide Web through Google or another search engine. I was delighted and even overwhelmed by how many such websites I found after only a few hours of exploring. I recommend that you explore too, because I found it wonderfully encouraging to see how many organizations now exist which support the vision of this book, and I am sure you will be similarly encouraged and excited.

Organizations which empower women (but may or may not have a web site) are also listed in this resource appendix, including a couple of retreat centers.

Finally, I list a few suggestions for magazines, music, and film or videos that I or others have found to be good resources for empowering women. More will be listed on the website as well.

BOOKS ("MUST READS")

Now It's Our Turn	by Alana Lyons
Millionth Circle	by Jean Shinoda Bolen
The Gender Knot	by Allan Johnson
Empowering Women	by Louise Hay
The Chalice and the Blade	by Riane Eisler
The Partnership Way	by Riane Eisler and David Loye
Calling the Circle	by Christina Baldwin
Women's Reality	by Anne Wilson Schaef
Real Power (3rd Edition)	by Janet O. Hagberg
Circle of Stones	by Judith Duerk
At the Root of This Longing	by Carol Flinders
Shakti Woman	by Vicki Noble
The Goddess Within	by Jennifer Barker Woolger & Roger J. Woolger
Women in the World's Religions	by Ursula King, ed.
Weaving the Visions	by Carol Christ and Judith Plaskow, ed.
Patriarchy as a Conceptual Trap	by Elizabeth Dodson Gray
Sisterhood is Global	by Robin Morgan, ed.
Cries of the Spirit	by Marilyn Sewell, ed.
The Gender Knot	by Allan G. Johnson

MORE BOOKS

The Feminine Mystique	by Betty Friedan
Reinventing Womanhood	by Carolyn Heilbrun
The Divine Feminine	by Andrew Harvey
Swallow's Nest	by Marchiene Rienstra
Dance of the Spirit	by Maria Harris
The Return of the Mother	by Andrew Harvey
A Room of Her Own	by Virginia Woolf
Dance of the Dissident Daughter	by Sue Monk Kidd
The Woman with the Alabaster Jar	by Starbird
The Price of Motherhood	by Ann Crittenden

THE FUTURE FOR WOMEN - A N.E.W. BOOK

Woman, Be Free	by Pat Gundry
All We're Meant to Be	by Letha Scanzoni and Nancy Hardesty
Women, Men, and the Bible	by Virginia Molenkott
Beyond Power	by Marilyn French
The Heroine's Journey	by Maureen Murdock
Feel the Fear & Do It Anyway	by Susan Jeffers
Woman and Nature	by Susan Griffin
Surfacing	by Margaret Atwood
Here All Dwell Free	by Gertrud Mueller Nelson
Coming Home	by Nelle Morton
You Are What You Say	by Karen Burton Mains
The Dance of Anger	by Harrier Goldhor Lerner
Fierce Tenderness	by Mary E. Hunt
Lift Every Voice	by Mary Potter Engel and Susan Thistelwaite, ed.
The Feminine Face of God	by Anderson and Hopkins
Creative Disobedience	by Dorothy Solee
A Life of One's Own	by Joanna Field
Omni Gender	by Virginia Molenkott
Women Who Run With the Wolves	by Clarissa Pinkola Estes

Note: Lindsay McKenna writes "trade" romantic novels with a difference; her heroines are always strong women, and they are linked with men in a way that models equal partnership between men and women. Silhouette publishes many of her titles.

SOME ORGANIZATIONS THAT EMPOWER WOMEN

American Association of University Women
1111 16th St. N.W. Washington, D.C. 20036 USA
phone: 202-785-7712

National Organization for Women Suite 700
1000 16th St. N.W. Washington, D.C. 20036

phone: 202-331-0066
The Fund for the Feminist Majority
1600 Wilson Blvd. Ste. 704, Arlington, VA 22209
phone: 703-522-2214

League of Women Voters
1730 M St. N.W. Suite 1000, Washington D.C. 20036
phone: 202-429-1965

Emily's List
805 15th St. N.W. Suite 400, Washington D.C. 20005

A.C.L.U. Women's Project
132 W. 43rd St. New York, New York 10036
phone: 212-944-9800

American Women's Economic Development Corp.
71 Vanderbilt Ave. New York, New York 10169
phone: 212-688-1900

Amnesty International USA Women and Human Rights Project
322 8th Ave. New York, New York. 10001
phone: 212-633-4200

National Coalition Vs. Domestic Violence
P.O. Box 34103, Washington, D.C. 20043
phone: 202-638-6388

Older Women's League
666 11th St. N.W. Washington, D.C. 20001
phone: 202-783-6686

U.S. Network for Women (empowering women worldwide)
633 Pennsylvania Ave., Washington, D.C. 20004
phone: 202-737-0121

THE FUTURE FOR WOMEN - A N.E.W. BOOK

Religious Network for Equality for Women (worldwide)
475 Riverside Drive, New York, N.Y. 10115

National Organization of Men Vs. Sexism (Box 5)
798 Pennsylvania Ave., Pittsburgh, PA 15221

9-5 Association of Working Women
238 West Wisconsin Ave. Milwaukee, WI 53202
phone: 414-274-0925

Women's Environment & Development Organization
355 Lexington Ave., 3rd floor, New York, N.Y. 10017
phone: 212-973-0325

Natural World Seminar: Self-empowerment for women who want to understand and utilize Mother Earth energy to help heal themselves.
Eileen Nauman, P.O.Box 2513, Cottonwood, Arizona 86326

MorningStar Adventures (A women's retreat center)
20564 Morningstar Trail, LeRoy, Michigan 49655
phone: 1-231-768-4368

National Women's History Museum
2760 Eisenhower Avenue, Suite 254, Alexandria, VA 22314

Women's Perspective on Money and Spirituality
421 Meadow Street, Fairfield, CT 06430
phone: 203-336-2238

Leaven
P.O. Box 23233, Lansing, MI 48909
phone: 989-855-2606

Witness and Women's Leadership Institute
161 Ottawa N.W., Waters Building, suite 305-C, Grand Rapids, MI 49503
phone: 616-459-7214

SOME WEBSITES THAT EMPOWER WOMEN

www.feminist.org
www.now.org
www.aauw.org
www.witnesschange.org
www.leaven.org
www.womensperspective.org
www.vday.org
www.gatherthewomen.org
www.networktoempowerwomen.org
www.womensperspective.org
www.reimaginingcommunity.org
www.water.org
www.peerspirit.com
www.utne.café.com/millionthcircle
www.internationalsisters.org
www.womensorganizations.org
www.euronet.nl

SOME MAGAZINES, MUSIC, & MOVIES THAT EMPOWER WOMEN

MS. Magazine; 230 Park Ave. New York, N.Y. 10169

Off Our Backs 2423 18th St. N.W. Washington, D.C. 2009

CD's: Jennifer Berezan: "She Who Hears the Cries of the World" and "Returning."
Kathryn Christian: "Holy Mother."

THE FUTURE FOR WOMEN - A N.E.W. BOOK

MOVIES/VIDEOS

Frida
Hours
Schreck
Thelma and Louise
Fried Green Tomatoes
Nine to Five
Tootsie
Legally Blonde
First Wives Club
Vagina Monologues
Mother Wove the Morning
Bend It Like Beckham

There are many, many more empowering resources. If you would like to add your favorites to these, visit the N.E.W. website (*www.networktoempowerwomen.org*) There will be web pages devoted to the listing of resources you suggest.

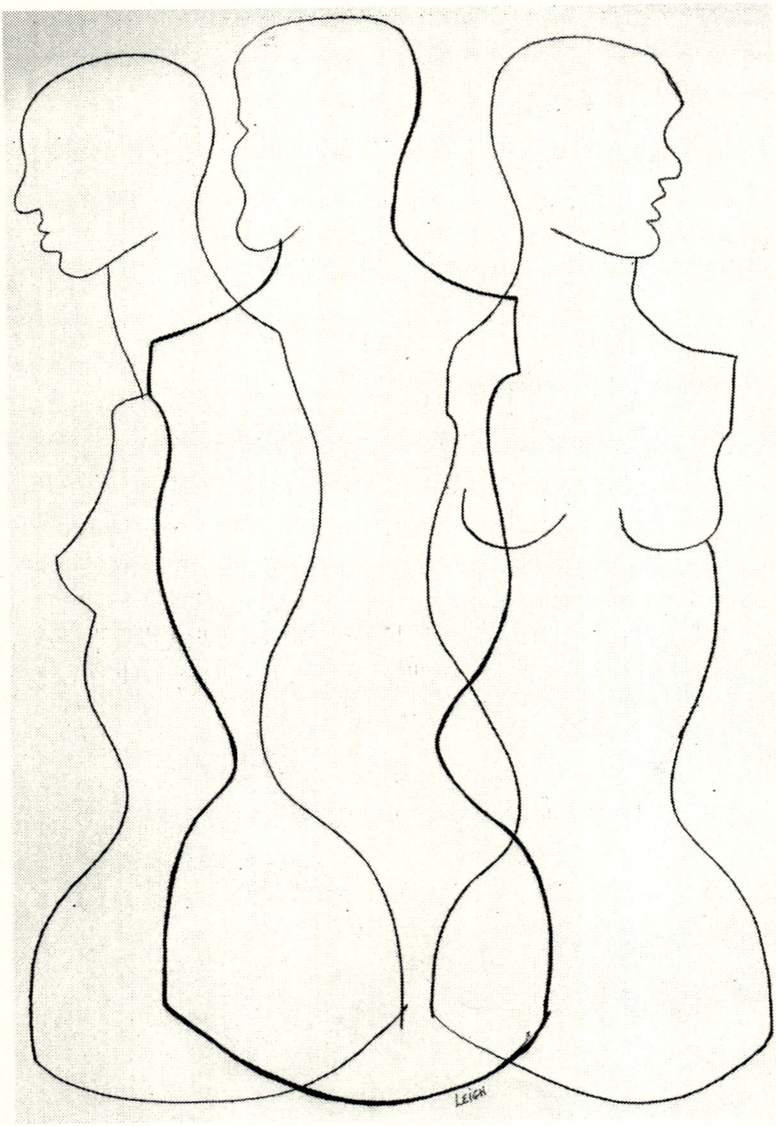
LEIGH

CIRCLE MEETING GUIDES

You are gladly given permission and warmly welcome to copy and use the N.E.W. Circle Meeting Guides printed below. And of course, you are invited to modify them as needed for your circle, so that they work for you.

Note: The leader of this meeting who chooses to use the suggested rituals will need to bring a candle, matches, a bell, a talking object, (ball, stone, stick, feather, flower, etc.) and a bowl of stones.

CIRCLE MEETING GUIDE: FIRST QUESTION MEETING

Welcome: Each woman says her name and why she has come.

Opening Ritual: The leader lights a candle or rings a bell, and leads the group in an opening moment of silence and centering.

Suggestion: Ask participants to take three deep breaths, close their eyes, and imagine Light filling each person, and the whole room. After a few moments of silence, invite them to open their eyes.

READING OF THE PURPOSE AND VISION, NINE AGREEMENTS, AND NINE QUESTIONS:

The leader hands out a printed copy of the Purpose and Vision for N.E.W., the Nine Agreements for circle process, and the Nine Questions. The leader and participants take turns reading them out loud. Questions and comments about these are welcome after the meeting is over. Alternatively, the leader or someone else present can simply read the material below out loud so everyone can hear.

THE PURPOSE AND VISION FOR N.E.W.

The purpose of the Network to Empower Women is to create and develop a circle-process and link women and resources on the World Wide Web in a way that enables the empowering of women everywhere.

Power is understood as the ability to help people and all of life flourish.

It has nothing to do with domination or control.

It does have to do with the ability to create, choose, and act for the flourishing of oneself and all creation.

Women need to be able to use their innate power for this purpose,

Women and men need to fly together in every arena of society, so that humanity can finally become like a bird that is flying because it is using both wings.

Women's gifts and wisdom are desperately needed if the world is to have a flourishing future.

The vision for N.E. W. is a worldwide network of circles that intentionally empower women, meeting in as many places as possible, linked with the many other resources and organizations already empowering women.

THE NINE AGREEMENTS FOR NEW CIRCLES

1. We meet in a circle with a Center that symbolizes the Wisdom within and among us.
2. We all listen as each one speaks in turn, using a symbolic object. We do not interrupt, cross talk, or give advice during the meeting.
3. We honor and respect the confidentiality of what is spoken in the circle.
4. We honor each one's contribution, listen without judgment, and support each other in a loving manner.
5. We all take responsibility for the process of the group, honoring time constraints and the agreements that guide the circle. Leadership is shared and rotated.
6. We exercise our personal right to refrain from any activity that violates our boundaries.
7. We all rely on the Wisdom of the circle's center and in each of us. The circle is like a wheel with each person connected to the hub at the center. To remain centered, we observe a brief silence between

each woman's reflections, and at any time during the meeting someone asks for it.
8. In between meetings, we connect with each other in order to help one another continue to explore the questions of the N.E.W. process, and offer support as needed. We especially reach out to those who are new to the circle meetings and process.
9. We want to reach out to as many women as possible in order to accomplish the vision of N.E.W. Therefore, we meet in a public location, safe, free of interruption, and open to any woman who wishes to attend.

We may collect a small fee at the meeting to defray any expenses.

The time frame can be as short as an hour once a week, or a couple Of hours once or twice a month.

We cover one of the Questions at each meeting, and repeat the Cycle of Nine Questions as often as desired.

Ideally, there are NEW circles meeting in many places at many times so that a woman can always find one when she wants it.

THE NINE QUESTION PROCESS (PARTICIPANTS MAY CHOOSE ONE OR MORE PARTS OF A QUESTION THAT HAS MORE THAN ONE PART.)

1. What am I grateful to have survived? Accomplished?
   Who or what has empowered me in my life so far?
2. What damaging, false beliefs about myself and/or women do I want to release?
   What healing, helpful beliefs do I want to affirm and live?
3. How have I found and followed my own Inner Authority?
   How will I continue to do so?
4. What are the spiritual practices and resources that empower me?
5. What obstacles to using my innate power as a woman have I/we encountered? What are some strategies for dealing with them?
   How do I stop giving away my power?
6. What can I imagine, and what do I want for my flourishing and the flourishing of all?

7. What concrete actions could I/we take to manifest what I/we want?
8. How can I live with greater connection and support with women and girls in my circles, community, and the world?
9. Free choice

EXPLORING QUESTION ONE:

What am I grateful to have survived? Accomplished?
Who or what has empowered me in my life so far?

A talking object, such as a stone, stick, feather, etc. is passed from woman to woman as each one speaks. While holding the object, each woman has an opportunity to reflect upon Question One. When she is done, she puts a stone in the center of the circle honoring someone who has empowered her.

After all have shared, an opportunity is given, if there is time, for those who have not spoken or wish to say something more to do so.

The meeting closes with a ritual of some kind: a song, a prayer, a moment of silence, etc.

Suggestion: The leader invites the women to stand together in a circle. She takes a stone and passes it around the circle, asking each woman to hold it in her hand and put the warmth of blessing energy into it. Then she passes the stone to the next woman, who receives its blessing energy as she holds it, adds her own to it, and passes it on, until it has gone around the circle.

The leader recites a blessing she chooses for the occasion. Each woman is then invited to take a stone from the table at the Center home with her and put it in a place that will remind her of the blessing and support of the circle.

Someone volunteers to lead the next circle meeting. All are encouraged to take a few moments before leaving to pair up and arrange for a way to connect with each other between meetings.

? ? ? ? ? ? ? ? ?

Note: The leader of the second meeting (see below) who chooses to use the suggested rituals will need to bring a candle, matches, a bell, a talking object, (ball, stone, stick, feather, flower, etc.) a fireproof container in which to burn paper, thin, easily burnable paper on which to write, and pencils or pens, a vase, and flowers for everyone. (Always have more than enough!)

CIRCLE MEETING GUIDE: SECOND QUESTION MEETING

Welcome: Each woman says her name and why she has come.

Opening Ritual: The leader lights a candle or rings a bell, and leads the group in an opening moment of silence and centering.

Suggestion: Ask participants to take three deep breaths, close their eyes, and imagine Light filling each person, and the whole room. After a few moments of silence, invite them to open their eyes.

READING OF THE PURPOSE AND VISION, NINE AGREEMENTS, AND NINE QUESTIONS:

The leader hands out a printed copy of the Purpose and Vision for N.E.W., the Nine Agreements for circle process, and the Nine Questions. The leader and participants take turns reading them out loud. Questions and comments about these are welcome after the meeting is over. Alternatively, the leader or someone else present can simply read the material below out loud so everyone can hear.

THE PURPOSE AND VISION FOR N.E.W.

The purpose of the Network to Empower Women is to create and develop a circle-process and link women and resources on the World Wide Web in a way that enables the empowering of women everywhere.

Power is understood as the ability to help people and all of life flourish.

It has nothing to do with domination or control.

It does have to do with the ability to create, choose, and act for the flourishing of oneself and all creation.

Women need to be able to use their innate power for this purpose,

Women and men need to fly together in every arena of society, so that humanity can finally become like a bird that is flying because it is using both wings.

Women's gifts and wisdom are desperately needed if the world is to have a flourishing future.

The vision for N.E. W. is a worldwide network of circles that intentionally empowers women, meeting in as many places as possible, linked with the many other resources and organizations already empowering women.

THE NINE AGREEMENTS FOR NEW CIRCLES

1. We meet in a circle with a Center that symbolizes the Wisdom within and among us.
2. We all listen as each one speaks in turn, using a symbolic object. We do not interrupt, cross talk, or give advice during the meeting.
3. We honor and respect the confidentiality of what is spoken in the circle.
4. We honor each one's contribution, listen without judgment, and support each other in a loving manner.
5. We all take responsibility for the process of the group, honoring time constraints and the agreements that guide the circle. Leadership is shared and rotated.
6. We exercise our personal right to refrain from any activity that violates our boundaries.
7. We all rely on the Wisdom of the circle's center and in each of us. The circle is like a wheel with each person connected to the hub at the center. To remain centered, we observe a brief silence between each woman's reflections, and at any time during the meeting someone asks for it.
8. In between meetings, we connect with each other in order to help one another continue to explore the questions of the N.E.W.

process, and offer support as needed. We especially reach out to those who are new to the circle meetings and process.

9. We want to reach out to as many women as possible in order to accomplish the vision of N.E.W. Therefore, we meet in a public location, safe, free of interruption, and open to any woman who wishes to attend.

We may collect a small fee at the meeting to defray any expenses.

The time frame can be as short as an hour once a week, or a couple of hours once or twice a month.

We cover one of the Questions at each meeting, and repeat the cycle of Nine Questions as often as desired.

Ideally, there are NEW circles meeting in many places at many times so that a woman can always find one when she needs it.

THE NINE QUESTION PROCESS (PARTICIPANTS MAY CHOOSE ONE OR MORE PARTS OF A QUESTION THAT HAS MORE THAN ONE PART.)

1. What am I grateful to have survived? Accomplished? Who or what has empowered me in my life so far?
2. What damaging, false beliefs about myself and/or women do I want to release?
What healing, helpful beliefs do I want to affirm and live?
3. How have I found and followed my own Inner Authority?
How will I continue to do so?
4. What are the spiritual practices and resources that empower me?
5. What obstacles to using my innate power as a woman have I/we encountered? What are some strategies for dealing with them?
How do I stop giving away my power?
6. What can I imagine, and what do I want for my flourishing and the flourishing of all?
7. What concrete actions could I/we take to manifest what I/we want?
8. How can I live with greater connection and support with women and girls in my circles, community, and the world?
9. Free choice

THE FUTURE FOR WOMEN - A N.E.W. BOOK

EXPLORING QUESTION TWO:

What damaging, false beliefs about myself and/or women do I want to release? What healing, helpful beliefs do I want to affirm and live?

Everyone is given a piece of paper that burns quickly and easily, and something to write with. After everyone has held the talking object and had a chance to reflect on the first half of this question, the talking object is placed in the Center while participants write down symbols or words of beliefs they would like to release. When all are ready, one at a time, each puts her paper in a fireproof container in the center, and lights a match to it.

When it has burned up, it is the next woman's turn. There is silence during this time.

Next, the talking object is passed around again, and each woman has a chance to reflect on the second part of the question. This time, when she is done, she takes a flower from a pile of flowers on the floor near the center, and places it in a vase that is in the Center.

When everyone has had a turn, there is a bouquet of flowers, and a container of ashes in the Center, symbolizing beliefs that have been released and beliefs that have been affirmed by each woman.

The meeting closes with a ritual of some kind: a song, a prayer, a moment of silence, etc.

Suggestion: The leader asks the women to stand together in a circle. She passes the vase of flowers around. Each woman takes her flower back out of the vase as it is passed around the circle so she can take it home and put it in a place that reminds her of the beliefs she and others in the circle have chosen to affirm and live. A song, prayer, quote, or blessing may be offered.

Someone volunteers to lead the next circle meeting. All are encouraged to take a few moments before leaving to pair up and arrange for a way to connect with each other between meetings.

? ? ? ? ? ? ? ? ?

Note: The leader of the third meeting (see below) who chooses to use the suggested rituals will need to bring a candle, matches, a bell, drum, or musical instrument, a talking object, (ball, stone, stick, feather, flower, etc) and enough small vigil lights or candles for all the participants.

CIRCLE MEETING GUIDE: THIRD QUESTION MEETING

Welcome: Each woman says her name and why she has come, or (briefly!) anything else she chooses.

Opening Ritual: The leader lights a candle, rings a bell, or drums, or plays a musical instrument to call the group together, and leads the group in an opening moment of silence and centering or a brief meditation suited to the question of the day.

Suggestion: Ask participants to take three deep breaths, close their eyes, and imagine Light filling each person, and the whole room. After a few moments of silence, invite them to open their eyes.

READING OF THE PURPOSE AND VISION, NINE AGREEMENTS, AND NINE QUESTIONS:

The leader hands out a printed copy of the Purpose and Vision for N.E.W., the Nine Agreements for circle process, and the Nine Questions. The leader and participants take turns reading them out loud. Questions and comments about these are welcome after the meeting is over. Alternatively, the leader or someone else present can simply read the material below out loud so everyone can hear.

THE PURPOSE AND VISION FOR N.E.W.

The purpose of the Network to Empower Women is to create and develop a circle-process and link women and resources on the world wide web in a way that enables the empowering of women everywhere.

Power is understood as the ability to help people and all of life flourish.

It has nothing to do with domination or control.

It does have to do with the ability to create, choose, and act for the flourishing of oneself and all creation.

Women need to be able to use their innate power for this purpose,

Women and men need to fly together in every arena of society, so that humanity can finally become like a bird that is flying because it is using both wings.

Women's gifts and wisdom are desperately needed if the world is to have a flourishing future.

The vision for N.E. W. is a worldwide network of circles that intentionally empowers women, meeting in as many places as possible, linked with the many other resources and organizations already empowering women.

The Nine Agreements for NEW Circles

1. We meet in a circle with a Center that symbolizes the Wisdom within and among us.
2. We all listen as each one speaks in turn, using a symbolic object. We do not interrupt, cross talk, or give advice during the meeting.
3. We honor and respect the confidentiality of what is spoken in the circle.
4. We honor each one's contribution, listen without judgment, and support each other in a loving manner.
5. We all take responsibility for the process of the group, honoring time constraints and the agreements that guide the circle. Leadership is shared and rotated.
6. We exercise our personal right to refrain from any activity that violates our boundaries.
7. We all rely on the Wisdom of the circle's center and in each of us. The circle is like a wheel with each person connected to the hub at the center. To remain centered, we observe a brief silence between each woman's reflections, and at any time during the meeting someone asks for it.

8. In between meetings, we connect with each other in order to help one another continue to explore the questions of the N.E.W. process, and offer support as needed. We especially reach out to those who are new to the circle meetings and process.
9. We want to reach out to as many women as possible in order to accomplish the vision of N.E.W. Therefore, we meet in a public location, safe, free of interruption, and open to any woman who wishes to attend. We may collect a small fee at the meeting to defray any expenses. The time frame can be as short as an hour once a week, or a couple of hours once or twice a month.

We cover one of the Questions at each meeting, and repeat the cycle of Nine Questions as often as desired.

Ideally, there are NEW circles meeting in many places at many times so that a woman can always find one when she wants it.

The Nine Question Process (Participants may choose one or more parts of a question that has more than one part.)

1. What am I grateful to have survived? Accomplished? Who or what has empowered me in my life so far?
2. What damaging, false beliefs about myself and/or women do I want to release?
What healing, helpful beliefs do I want to affirm and live?
3. How have I found and followed my own Inner Authority? How will I continue to do so?
4. What are the spiritual practices and resources that empower me?
5. What obstacles to using my innate power as a woman have I/we encountered? What are some strategies for dealing with them? How do I stop giving away my power?
6. What can I imagine, and what do I want for my flourishing and the flourishing of all?
7. What concrete actions could I/we take to manifest what I/we want?
8. How can I live with greater connection and support with women and girls in my circles, community, and the world?
9. Free choice

EXPLORING QUESTION THREE:

How have I found and followed my own Inner Authority?
How will I continue to do so?

In the Center there is a ring of small candles, or vigil lights, arranged around a larger central candle. The leader starts the talking object going around the circle. After each woman holds the object and responds to Question Three, she lights one of the little candles from the big candle as a symbol of her inner authority and its connection to the Wisdom that shines in every woman. When everyone has had a chance to respond to the question and light a candle, the circle sits in silence, absorbing the lights they have lit and what they mean.

The meeting closes with a ritual of some kind: a song, a prayer, a moment of silence, etc.

Suggestion: The leader asks the women to stand together in a circle. She asks them to hold their candles high above their heads while singing "This little light of mine, I'm gonna let it shine" or some other appropriate song. Or, a quote or prayer may be offered that reflects the light of women's authority and wisdom.

Someone volunteers to lead the next circle meeting. (Note: not every woman has to take a turn leading, but it is important that leadership is rotated and shared by at least some of the women, so that the circle does not become dominated by one leader.) All are encouraged to take a few moments before leaving to pair up and arrange for a way to connect with each other between meetings.

? ? ? ? ? ? ? ? ?

Note: The leader of the fourth meeting (see below) who chooses to use the suggested rituals will need to bring a candle, matches, a bell, drum, or musical instrument, a talking object, (ball, stone, stick, feather, flower, etc) a little bowl of seeds (sunflower seeds work well, but use whatever is available) and a container with soil in it for each participant. Mugs, small clay pots, little baskets with lining to keep the moisture in—all work well. (Check the local flea market or ask around for cups no one wants to save expense)

CIRCLE MEETING GUIDE: FOURTH QUESTION MEETING

Welcome: Each woman says her name and why she has come, or (briefly!) anything else she chooses.

Opening Ritual: The leader lights a candle, rings a bell, or drums, or plays a musical instrument to call the group together, and leads the group in an opening moment of silence and centering or a brief meditation suited to the question of the day.

Suggestion: Everyone stands and takes three deep breaths, in through the nose, and out through the mouth, with eyes closed. Then everyone imagines that there are silver roots growing from the soles of their feet deep down into Mother Earth—300 feet or more.

After a few moments of silence, all are seated.

READING OF THE PURPOSE AND VISION, NINE AGREEMENTS, AND NINE QUESTIONS:

The leader hands out a printed copy of the Purpose and Vision for N.E.W., the Nine Agreements for circle process, and the Nine Questions. The leader and participants take turns reading them out loud. Questions and comments about these are welcome after the meeting is over. Alternatively, the leader or someone else present can simply read the material below out loud so everyone can hear.

THE PURPOSE AND VISION FOR N.E.W.

The purpose of the Network to Empower Women is to create and develop a circle-process and link women and resources on the World Wide Web in a way that enables the empowering of women everywhere.

Power is understood as the ability to help people and all of life flourish.

It has nothing to do with domination or control.

It does have to do with the ability to create, choose, and act for the flourishing of oneself and all creation.

Women need to be able to use their innate power for this purpose,

Women and men need to fly together in every arena of society, so that humanity can finally become like a bird that is flying because it is using both wings.

Women's gifts and wisdom are desperately needed if the world is to have a flourishing future.

The vision for N.E. W. is a worldwide network of circles that intentionally empower women, meeting in as many places as possible, linked with the many other resources and organizations already empowering women.

THE NINE AGREEMENTS FOR NEW CIRCLES

1. We meet in a circle with a Center that symbolizes the Wisdom within and among us.
2. We all listen as each one speaks in turn, using a symbolic object. We do not interrupt, cross talk, or give advice during the meeting.
3. We honor and respect the confidentiality of what is spoken in the circle.
4. We honor each one's contribution, listen without judgment, and support each other in a loving manner.
5. We all take responsibility for the process of the group, honoring time constraints and the agreements that guide the circle. Leadership is shared and rotated.
6. We exercise our personal right to refrain from any activity that violates our boundaries.
7. We all rely on the Wisdom of the circle's center and in each of us. The circle is like a wheel with each person connected to the hub at the center. To remain centered, we observe a brief silence between each woman's reflections, and at any time during the meeting someone asks for it.

8. In between meetings, we connect with each other in order to help one another continue to explore the questions of the N.E.W. process, and offer support as needed. We especially reach out to those who are new to the circle meetings and process.
9. We want to reach out to as many women as possible in order to accomplish the vision of N.E.W. Therefore, we meet in a public location, safe, free of interruption, and open to any woman who wishes to attend.

We may collect a small fee at the meeting to defray any expenses.

The time frame can be as short as an hour once a week, or a couple

Of hours once or twice a month.

We cover one of the Questions at each meeting, and repeat the cycle of Nine Questions as often as desired.

Ideally, there are NEW circles meeting in many places at many times so that a woman can always find one when she wants it.

THE NINE QUESTION PROCESS (PARTICIPANTS MAY CHOOSE ONE OR MORE PARTS OF A QUESTION THAT HAS MORE THAN ONE PART.)

1. What am I grateful to have survived? Accomplished? Who or what has empowered me in my life so far?
2. What damaging, false beliefs about myself and/or women do I want to release?
What healing, helpful beliefs do I want to affirm and live?
3. How have I found and followed my own Inner Authority? How will I continue to do so?
4. What are the spiritual practices and resources that empower me?
5. What obstacles to using my innate power as a woman have I/we encountered? What are some strategies for dealing with them? How do I stop giving away my power?
6. What can I imagine, and what do I want for my flourishing and the flourishing of all?
7. What concrete actions could I/we take to manifest what I/we want?

8. How can I live with greater connection and support with women and girls in my circles, community, and the world?
9. Free choice

EXPLORING QUESTION FOUR:

What are the spiritual practices and resources that empower me?
   The leader passes a talking object around the circle, inviting each woman to respond to this question as she holds it, and the others silently listen. There is one container for each person, filled with soil, and a pile of seeds in the Center. After each woman speaks, she plants sunflower (or other type) seeds in a little container that has soil in it, leaving it in the Center.
   When everyone has had a chance to speak, each of the women takes her container of seeds as a sign of her commitment to use the spiritual practices and resources that empower her. The leader encourages each woman to take the container home and keep it in a place where she will water it, watch it grow, and let it remind her to let her commitment grow and blossom.
   The meeting closes with a song, a prayer, a moment of silence, etc.

Someone volunteers to lead the next circle meeting. (Note: Not every woman has to take a turn leading, but it is important that leadership is rotated and shared by at least some of the women, so that the circle does not become dominated by one leader.) All are encouraged to take a few moments before leaving to pair up and arrange for a way to connect with each other between meetings.

? ? ? ? ? ? ? ? ?

Note: The leader of the fifth meeting (see below) who chooses to use the suggested rituals will need to bring a candle, matches, a bell, drum, or musical instrument, a talking object, which in this case is a small bowl or glass or chalice of perfumed oil which will also be used for the ritual association with Question Five.

CIRCLE MEETING GUIDE: FIFTH QUESTION MEETING

Welcome: Each woman says her name and why she has come, or (briefly!) anything else she chooses.

Opening Ritual: The leader lights a candle, rings a bell, or drums, or plays a musical instrument to call the group together, and leads the group in an opening moment of silence and centering or a brief meditation suited to the question of the day.

Suggestion: The leader asks everyone to take a couple deep breaths, close their eyes, and relax. Then she says, "Imagine you are in a race. You are at the starting line, looking down the racetrack ahead of you, anticipating the run. As you leave the starting line and round the first turn of the track, you notice a series of hurdles in front of you. You were not expecting them, but you realize you have to jump over them to continue the race. You keep running towards them while in your mind's eye you see yourself leaping easily over each of them. And you do! You can feel the wind in your hair as your legs clear the hurdles with room to spare, and you continue on your race. You run with great exhilaration, because you were able to take the hurdles in stride. Feel the exhilaration. Stay with the feeling . . . . Now, gradually come back to the present, take a couple deep breaths, and open your eyes."

When all are ready, the leader begins the rest of the meeting.

READING OF THE PURPOSE AND VISION, NINE AGREEMENTS, AND NINE QUESTIONS:

The leader hands out a printed copy of the Purpose and Vision for N.E.W., the Nine Agreements for circle process, and the Nine Questions. The leader and participants take turns reading them out loud. Questions and comments about these are welcome after the meeting is over. Alternatively, the leader or someone else present can simply read the material below out loud so everyone can hear.

THE FUTURE FOR WOMEN - A N.E.W. BOOK

The Purpose and Vision for N.E.W.

The purpose of the Network to Empower Women is to create and develop a circle-process and link women and resources on the world wide web in a way that enables the empowering of women everywhere.

Power is understood as the ability to help people and all of life flourish.

It has nothing to do with domination or control.

It does have to do with the ability to create, choose, and act for the flourishing of oneself and all creation.

Women need to be able to use their innate power for this purpose,

Women and men need to fly together in every arena of society, so that humanity can finally become like a bird that is flying because it is using both wings.

Women's gifts and wisdom are desperately needed if the world is to have a flourishing future.

The vision for N.E.W. is a worldwide network of circles that intentionally empower women, meeting in as many places as possible, linked with the many other resources and organizations already empowering women.

The Nine Agreements for NEW Circles

1. We meet in a circle with a Center that symbolizes the Wisdom within and among us.
2. We all listen as each one speaks in turn, using a symbolic object. We do not interrupt, cross talk, or give advice during the meeting.
3. We honor and respect the confidentiality of what is spoken in the circle.
4. We honor each one's contribution, listen without judgment, and support each other in a loving manner.
5. We all take responsibility for the process of the group, honoring time constraints and the agreements that guide the circle. Leadership is shared and rotated.
6. We exercise our personal right to refrain from any activity that violates our boundaries.

7. We all rely on the Wisdom of the circle's center and in each of us. The circle is like a wheel with each person connected to the hub at the center. To remain centered, we observe a brief silence between each woman's reflections, and at any time during the meeting someone asks for it.

   In between meetings, we connect with each other in order to help one another continue to explore the questions of the N.E.W. process, and offer support as needed. We especially reach out to those who are new to the circle meetings and process.

8. We want to reach out to as many women as possible in order to accomplish the vision of N.E.W. Therefore, we meet in a public location, safe, free of interruption, and open to any woman who wishes to attend.

   We may collect a small fee at the meeting to defray any expenses.

   The time frame can be as short as an hour once a week, or a couple of hours once or twice a month. We cover one of the Questions at each meeting, and repeat the cycle of Nine Questions as often as desired.

   Ideally, there are NEW circles meeting in many places at many times so that a woman can always find one when she needs it.

THE NINE QUESTION PROCESS (PARTICIPANTS MAY CHOOSE ONE OR MORE PARTS OF A QUESTION THAT HAS MORE THAN ONE PART.)

1. What am I grateful to have survived? Accomplished? Who or what has empowered me in my life so far?
2. What damaging, false beliefs about myself and/or women do I want to release?
   What healing, helpful beliefs do I want to affirm and live?
3. How have I found and followed my own Inner Authority? How will I continue to do so?
4. What are the spiritual practices and resources that empower me?
5. What obstacles to using my innate power as a woman have I/we encountered? What are some strategies for dealing with them? How do I stop giving away my power?

6. What can I imagine, and what do I want for my flourishing and the flourishing of all?
7. What concrete actions could I/we take to manifest what I/we want?
8. How can I live with greater connection and support with women and girls in my circles, community, and the world?
9. Free choice

EXPLORING QUESTION FIVE:

What obstacles to using my innate power as a woman have I/we encountered? What are some strategies for dealing with them?
How do I stop giving away my power?

There is a small bowl, cup, or chalice of perfumed oil in the Center of the circle. The leader takes the container as the talking object for the exploring of Question Five.

As each woman speaks, she holds the container of oil in her hands. When she is done, the other women in the circle come up to her, one by one, and in silence anoint her with a spiral on the forehead, throat, hands, top of head, or wherever the woman holding the oil prefers. She receives this anointing as an empowering blessing, and a sign of Divine Authority to do what she had been gifted and led to do and be. The anointed woman then passes the bowl to the woman next to her, and the process is repeated. When everyone has had a chance to speak, and has been anointed, all the women stand and together dip their finger in the container of oil in the Center of the circle, turn outward facing the world, and make a spiral in the air with their oiled finger. This is a sign of blessing the world with women's power, and of moving freely through any obstacles around the spiral of their power.

Finally, all face each other in a circle again, and holding hands sing "We shall Overcome" or another suitable song or chant. The leader may substitute or add a quote, or prayer or affirmations on overcoming obstacles

Someone volunteers to lead the next circle meeting. (Note: Not every woman has to take a turn leading, but it is important that leadership is rotated and shared by at least some of the women, so that the circle does not become dominated by one leader.) All are encouraged to take a few moments before leaving to pair up and arrange for a way to connect with each other between meetings.

? ? ? ? ? ? ? ? ?

Note: The leader of the sixth meeting (see below) who chooses to use the suggested rituals will need to bring a candle, matches, a bell, drum, or musical instrument, a talking object, which in this case is a ball of clay about the size of a peach or large lemon, plain paper and crayons, markers, pastels or whatever is available for drawing.

CIRCLE MEETING GUIDE: SIXTH QUESTION MEETING

Welcome: Each woman says her name and why she has come, or (briefly!) anything else she chooses.

Opening Ritual: The leader lights a candle, rings a bell, or drums, or plays a musical instrument to call the group together, and leads the group in an opening moment of silence and centering or a brief meditation suited to the question of the day.

Suggestion: The leader asks the women to close their eyes, take a few deep breaths and relax. Then she says, "Imagine that you had the power to make this world just the way you wanted it to be. Now, what would that world be like? Imagine it as vividly as you can. (Pause for a little while.) Now, imagine your own life the way you would love to have it be. What would it look like? Imagine it as vividly and concretely as you can. (Another pause for a few moments.) When you are ready, open your eyes, and if you can, keep those images in the background of your mind as we go through out meeting today."

READING OF THE PURPOSE AND VISION, NINE AGREEMENTS, AND NINE QUESTIONS:

The leader hands out a printed copy of the Purpose and Vision for

N.E.W., the Nine Agreements for circle process, and the Nine Questions. The leader and participants take turns reading them out loud. Questions and comments about these are welcome after the meeting is over. Alternatively, the leader or someone else present can simply read the material below out loud so everyone can hear.

The Purpose and Vision for N.E.W.

The purpose of the Network to Empower Women is to create and develop a circle-process and link women and resources on the World Wide Web in a way that enables the empowering of women everywhere.

Power is understood as the ability to help people and all of life flourish.

It has nothing to do with domination or control.

It does have to do with the ability to create, choose, and act for the flourishing of oneself and all creation.

Women need to be able to use their innate power for this purpose,

Women and men need to fly together in every arena of society, so that humanity can finally become like a bird that is flying because it is using both wings.

Women's gifts and wisdom are desperately needed if the world is to have a flourishing future.

The vision for N.E. W. is a worldwide network of circles that intentionally empowers women, meeting in as many places as possible, linked with the many other resources and organizations already empowering women.

The Nine Agreements for NEW Circles

1. We meet in a circle with a Center that symbolizes the Wisdom within and among us.
2. We all listen as each one speaks in turn, using a symbolic object. We do not interrupt, cross talk, or give advice during the meeting.
3. We honor and respect the confidentiality of what is spoken in the circle.
4. We honor each one's contribution, listen without judgment, and support each other in a loving manner.

5. We all take responsibility for the process of the group, honoring time constraints and the agreements that guide the circle. Leadership is shared and rotated.
6. We exercise our personal right to refrain from any activity that violates our boundaries.
7. We all rely on the Wisdom of the circle's center and in each of us. The circle is like a wheel with each person connected to the hub at the center. To remain centered, we observe a brief silence between each woman's reflections, and at any time during the meeting someone asks for it.
8. In between meetings, we connect with each other in order to help one another continue to explore the questions of the N.E.W. process, and offer support as needed. We especially reach out to those who are new to the circle meetings and process.
9. We want to reach out to as many women as possible in order to accomplish the vision of N.E.W. Therefore, we meet in a public location, safe, free of interruption, and open to any woman who wishes to attend.

   We may collect a small fee at the meeting to defray any expenses.

   The time frame can be as short as an hour once a week, or a couple Of hours once or twice a month.

   We cover one of the Questions at each meeting, and repeat the cycle of Nine Questions as often as desired.

   Ideally, there are NEW circles meeting in many places at many times so that a woman can always find one when she wants it.

THE NINE QUESTION PROCESS (PARTICIPANTS MAY CHOOSE ONE OR MORE PARTS OF A QUESTION THAT HAS MORE THAN ONE PART.)

1. What am I grateful to have survived? Accomplished? Who or what has empowered me in my life so far?
2. What damaging, false beliefs about myself and/or women do I want to release?
   What healing, helpful beliefs do I want to affirm and live?

3. How have I found and followed my own Inner Authority? How will I continue to do so?
4. What are the spiritual practices and resources that empower me?
5. What obstacles to using my innate power as a woman have I/we encountered? What are some strategies for dealing with them? How do I stop giving away my power?
6. What can I imagine, and what do I want for my flourishing and the flourishing of all?
7. What concrete actions could I/we take to manifest what I/we want?
8. How can I live with greater connection and support with women and girls in my circles, community, and the world?
9. Free choice

EXPLORING QUESTION SIX:

What can I imagine, and what do I want, for my flourishing, and the flourishing of all?

First, in silence, each woman draws a simple picture or symbols of what she imagines and wants for her flourishing and the flourishing of all. Paper and crayons, or markers, or pastels, etc. are available at the Center of the circle. When everyone is done, each woman holds a ball of clay as she responds to Question Six. If she wishes, she may use her drawing as part of her sharing—or not. When each woman finishes talking, she gives the clay ball a little squeeze to leave her imprint on it, and then passes it to the next woman. When everyone has had a chance to hold the clay ball and share, the clay ball will have on it the imprints of all the women. It is placed in the Center to symbolize how we can all mold the future together.

   Suggested closing ritual. All the women join hands and raise them up as they look upward as if a huge dome above them on which they project with the eyes of their imagination the wants and hopes they have shared. After a few moments gazing above at their visions, the women let go of each other's hands and each woman takes a piece of the clay ball to take home and keep in a place that will remind her of what she and the circle have imagined for the flourishing of all. The leader may close with a fitting song, prayer, or reading.

Someone volunteers to lead the next circle meeting. (Note: Not every woman has to take a turn leading, but it is important that leadership is rotated and shared by at least some of the women, so that the circle does not become dominated by one leader.) All are encouraged to take a few moments before leaving to pair up and arrange for a way to connect with each other between meetings.

? ? ? ? ? ? ? ? ?

Note: The leader of the seventh meeting (see below) who chooses to use the suggested rituals will need to bring a candle, matches, and a bell, small drum, or a rattle. One of these will be used as a talking object. You will also need a small plate or bowl with stones for everyone.

CIRCLE MEETING GUIDE: SEVENTH QUESTION MEETING

Welcome: Each woman says her name and why she has come, or (briefly!) anything else she chooses.

Opening Ritual: The leader lights a candle, rings a bell, or drums, or plays a musical instrument to call the group together, and leads the group in an opening moment of silence and centering or a brief meditation suited to the question of the day.

READING OF THE PURPOSE AND VISION, NINE AGREEMENTS, AND NINE QUESTIONS:

The leader hands out a printed copy of the Purpose and Vision for N.E.W., the Nine Agreements for circle process, and the Nine Questions. The leader and participants take turns reading them out loud. Questions and comments about these are welcome after the meeting is over. Alternatively, the leader or someone else present can simply read the material below out loud so everyone can hear.

THE FUTURE FOR WOMEN - A N.E.W. BOOK

The Purpose and Vision for N.E.W.

The purpose of the Network to Empower Women is to create and develop a circle-process and link women and resources on the World Wide Web in a way that enables the empowering of women everywhere.

Power is understood as the ability to help people and all of life flourish.

It has nothing to do with domination or control.

It does have to do with the ability to create, choose, and act for the flourishing of oneself and all creation.

Women need to be able to use their innate power for this purpose,

Women and men need to fly together in every arena of society, so that humanity can finally become like a bird that is flying because it is using both wings.

Women's gifts and wisdom are desperately needed if the world is to have a flourishing future.

The vision for N.E. W. is a worldwide network of circles that intentionally empowers women, meeting in as many places as possible, linked with the many other resources and organizations already empowering women.

The Nine Agreements for NEW Circles

1. We meet in a circle with a Center that symbolizes the Wisdom within and among us.
2. We all listen as each one speaks in turn, using a symbolic object. We do not interrupt, cross talk, or give advice during the meeting.
3. We honor and respect the confidentiality of what is spoken in the circle.
4. We honor each one's contribution, listen without judgment, and support each other in a loving manner.
5. We all take responsibility for the process of the group, honoring time constraints and the agreements that guide the circle. Leadership is shared and rotated.
6. We exercise our personal right to refrain from any activity that violates our boundaries.

7. We all rely on the Wisdom of the circle's center and in each of us. The circle is like a wheel with each person connected to the hub at the center. To remain centered, we observe a brief silence between each woman's reflections, and at any time during the meeting someone asks for it.
8. In between meetings, we connect with each other in order to help one another continue to explore the questions of the N.E.W. process, and offer support as needed. We especially reach out to those who are new to the circle meetings and process.
9. We want to reach out to as many women as possible in order to accomplish the vision of N.E.W. Therefore, we meet in a public location, safe, free of interruption, and open to any woman who wishes to attend.

We may collect a small fee at the meeting to defray any expenses.

The time frame can be as short as an hour once a week, or a couple of hours once or twice a month.

We cover one of the Questions at each meeting, and repeat the cycle of Nine Questions as often as desired.

Ideally, there are NEW circles meeting in many places at many times so that a woman can always find one when she wants it.

THE NINE QUESTION PROCESS (PARTICIPANTS MAY CHOOSE ONE OR MORE PARTS OF A QUESTION THAT HAS MORE THAN ONE PART.)

1. What am I grateful to have survived? Accomplished? Who or what has empowered me in my life so far?
2. What damaging, false beliefs about myself and/or women do I want to release?
   What healing, helpful beliefs do I want to affirm and live?
3. How have I found and followed my own Inner Authority? How will I continue to do so?
4. What are the spiritual practices and resources that empower me?
5. What obstacles to using my innate power as a woman have I/we encountered? What are some strategies for dealing with them? How do I stop giving away my power?

6. What can I imagine, and what do I want for my flourishing and the flourishing of all?
7. What concrete actions could I/we take to manifest what I/we want?
8. How can I live with greater connection and support with women and girls in my circles, community, and the world?
9. Free choice

EXPLORING QUESTION SEVEN:

What concrete actions could I/we take to manifest what I/we want and need?

Suggested ritual: The leader shakes a rattle, rings a bell, or beats a drum several times.

Then, in silence, each woman takes paper and pencil or pen from the Center and listens to her inner Wisdom to help her respond to this question. She writes down what she hears in the silence. It could be words, or feelings, or images, or just a knowing. When everyone is done writing what they have "heard," the bell, drum, or rattle is passed as the talking object of the day. As each woman holds it, she responds to Question Seven, and if she wishes, shares what she heard in the silence. When everyone has had a chance to speak, the bell, drum, or rattle is passed around again, and each woman makes a sound with it to express her commitment to the actions she is willing to take.

To close, each woman takes a stone from a bowl in the Center to remind her of her commitment, and of how women can build a new and better future together, one commitment at a time, stone upon stone. The leader may offer a song, prayer, or quote to end the meeting.

Someone volunteers to lead the next circle meeting. (Note: Not every woman has to take a turn leading, but it is important that leadership is rotated and shared by at least some of the women, so that the circle does not become dominated by one leader.) All are encouraged to take a few moments before leaving to pair up and arrange for a way to connect with each other between meetings.

? ? ? ? ? ? ? ? ?

Note: The leader of the eighth meeting (see below) who chooses to use the suggested rituals will need to bring a candle, matches, a bell, small drum, rattle, or other musical instrument, and a good sized ball of ribbon, yarn, or string, which will be used as the talking object.

CIRCLE MEETING GUIDE: EIGHTH QUESTION MEETING

Welcome: Each woman says her name and why she has come, or (briefly!) anything else she chooses.

Opening Ritual: The leader lights a candle, rings a bell, or drums, or plays a musical instrument to call the group together, and leads the group in an opening moment of silence and centering or a brief meditation suited to the question of the day.

Suggestion: The leader asks the women to close their eyes, take a few deep breaths, and relax. Then she says, "Imagine the faces of the women and girls you know. See them before you, starting with those you know best. Look deeply, with love, into each one's eyes as you see them in your mind's eye. (Pause) Now, imagine women and girls you have never met, in places you have never been. Remember the images of women and girls in Asia, Africa, Europe, South America, and elsewhere, which you have seen on television or in the newspapers and magazines. As you recall them in your mind's eye, once again imagine looking deeply with love into each one's eyes. (Pause) When you are ready, open your eyes and bring your awareness back to the room."

READING OF THE PURPOSE AND VISION, NINE AGREEMENTS, AND NINE QUESTIONS:

The leader hands out a printed copy of the Purpose and Vision for N.E.W., the Nine Agreements for circle process, and the Nine Questions. The leader and participants take turns reading them out loud. Questions and comments about these are welcome after the meeting is over.

Alternatively, the leader or someone else present can simply read the material below out loud so everyone can hear.

The Purpose and Vision for N.E.W.

The purpose of the Network to Empower Women is to create and develop a circle-process and link women and resources on the World Wide Web in a way that enables the empowering of women everywhere.

Power is understood as the ability to help people and all of life flourish.

It has nothing to do with domination or control.

It does have to do with the ability to create, choose, and act for the flourishing of oneself and all creation.

Women need to be able to use their innate power for this purpose,

Women and men need to fly together in every arena of society, so that humanity can finally become like a bird that is flying because it is using both wings.

Women's gifts and wisdom are desperately needed if the world is to have a flourishing future.

The vision for N.E. W. is a worldwide network of circles that intentionally empowers women, meeting in as many places as possible, linked with the many other resources and organizations already empowering women.

The Nine Agreements for NEW Circles

1. We meet in a circle with a Center that symbolizes the Wisdom within and among us.
2. We all listen as each one speaks in turn, using a symbolic object. We do not interrupt, cross talk, or give advice during the meeting.
3. We honor and respect the confidentiality of what is spoken in the circle.
4. We honor each one's contribution, listen without judgment, and support each other in a loving manner.
5. We all take responsibility for the process of the group, honoring

time constraints and the agreements that guide the circle. Leadership is shared and rotated.
6. We exercise our personal right to refrain from any activity that violates our boundaries.
7. We all rely on the Wisdom of the circle's center and in each of us. The circle is like a wheel with each person connected to the hub at the center. To remain centered, we observe a brief silence between each woman's reflections, and at any time during the meeting someone asks for it.
8. In between meetings, we connect with each other in order to help one another continue to explore the questions of the N.E.W. process, and offer support as needed. We especially reach out to those who are new to the circle meetings and process.
9. We want to reach out to as many women as possible in order to accomplish the vision of N.E.W. Therefore, we meet in a public location, safe, free of interruption, and open to any woman who wishes to attend.

We may collect a small fee at the meeting to defray any expenses.

The time frame can be as short as an hour once a week, or a couple of hours once or twice a month.

We cover one of the Questions at each meeting, and repeat the cycle of Nine Questions as often as desired.

Ideally, there are NEW circles meeting in many places at many times so that a woman can always find one when she wants it.

THE NINE QUESTION PROCESS (PARTICIPANTS MAY CHOOSE ONE OR MORE PARTS OF A QUESTION THAT HAS MORE THAN ONE PART.)

1. What am I grateful to have survived? Accomplished? Who or what has empowered me in my life so far?
2. What damaging, false beliefs about myself and/or women do I want to release?
What healing, helpful beliefs do I want to affirm and live?
3. How have I found and followed my own Inner Authority? How will I continue to do so?

4. What are the spiritual practices and resources that empower me?
5. What obstacles to using my innate power as a woman have I/we encountered? What are some strategies for dealing with them? How do I stop giving away my power?
6. What can I imagine, and what do I want for my flourishing and the flourishing of all?
7. What concrete actions could I/we take to manifest what I/we want?
8. How can I live with greater connection and support with women and girls in my circles, community, and the world?
9. Free choice

Exploring Question Eight:

How can I live with greater connection and support with women and girls in my circles, community, and the world?

Suggested ritual: A ball of yarn, ribbon, or string is used as the talking object. Each one takes it and speaks in response to Question Eight. Then she winds the material around her hand several times. When she is finished, she passes it on to the next woman, who in turn holds it as she speaks, then winds some of the material around her hand several times, and on it goes, until everyone has had a chance to speak. When everyone is finished, all will be connected with the yarn, ribbon, or string. All sit for a few moments in silence, feeling their connection.

In closing, the leader cuts the string/yarn/ribbon between each woman. What remains around each one's wrist is to be taken home as a reminder of her commitment to make supportive connections with women and girls where she lives and out into the world.

The leader may close with a song such as "Weave, weave, weave us together" or some other appropriate song, prayer, affirmation, or reading

Someone volunteers to lead the next circle meeting. (Note: Not every woman has to take a turn leading, but it is important that leadership is rotated and shared by at least some of the women, so that the circle does not become dominated by one leader.) All are encouraged to take a few moments before leaving to pair up and arrange for a way to connect with each other between meetings.

Note: Everyone is encouraged to come to the next meeting on the Ninth Question, which is "free choice" with the question each would choose for herself, so that all can benefit from hearing each one's choice. It would be a nice idea for each one who comes to bring some symbol of her choice as well to use as part of her sharing and put in the Center.

? ? ? ? ? ? ? ? ?

Note: The leader of the ninth meeting (see below) who chooses to use the suggested rituals will need to bring a candle, matches, a bell, small drum, rattle, or other musical instrument, and a bowl of boiled eggs for everyone, along with crayons, markers, or whatever is available with which to draw on the eggs. Add whatever the circle has decided they want for a concluding celebration!

CIRCLE MEETING GUIDE: NINTH QUESTION MEETING

Welcome: Each woman says her name and why she has come, or (briefly!) anything else she chooses.

Opening Ritual: The leader lights a candle, rings a bell, or drums, or plays a musical instrument to call the group together, and leads the group in an opening moment of silence and centering or a brief meditation suited to the question of the day.

Suggestion: The leader lights a candle, and invites everyone to take its light into their bodies with their eyes, then close their eyes and imagine that light filling everyone, the whole room, and then the whole world with joy and peace. Everyone breathes deeply together for a while as they imagine this Light everywhere. After a few moments of silence, the leader invites everyone to open their eyes.

READING OF THE PURPOSE AND VISION, NINE AGREEMENTS, AND NINE QUESTIONS:

The leader hands out a printed copy of the Purpose and Vision for

N.E.W., the Nine Agreements for circle process, and the Nine Questions. The leader and participants take turns reading them out loud. Questions and comments about these are welcome after the meeting is over. Alternatively, the leader or someone else present can simply read the material below out loud so everyone can hear.

The Purpose and Vision for N.E.W.

The purpose of the Network to Empower Women is to create and develop a circle-process and link women and resources on the World Wide Web in a way that enables the empowering of women everywhere.

Power is understood as the ability to help people and all of life flourish.

It has nothing to do with domination or control.

It does have to do with the ability to create, choose, and act for the flourishing of oneself and all creation.

Women need to be able to use their innate power for this purpose,

Women and men need to fly together in every arena of society, so that humanity can finally become like a bird that is flying because it is using both wings.

Women's gifts and wisdom are desperately needed if the world is to have a flourishing future.

The vision for N.E. W. is a worldwide network of circles that intentionally empowers women, meeting in as many places as possible, linked with the many other resources and organizations already empowering women.

The Nine Agreements for NEW Circles

1. We meet in a circle with a Center that symbolizes the Wisdom within and among us.
2. We all listen as each one speaks in turn, using a symbolic object. We do not interrupt, cross talk, or give advice during the meeting.
3. We honor and respect the confidentiality of what is spoken in the circle.

4. We honor each one's contribution, listen without judgment, and support each other in a loving manner.
5. We all take responsibility for the process of the group, honoring time constraints and the agreements that guide the circle. Leadership is shared and rotated.
6. We exercise our personal right to refrain from any activity that violates our boundaries.
7. We all rely on the Wisdom of the circle's center and in each of us. The circle is like a wheel with each person connected to the hub at the center. To remain centered, we observe a brief silence between each woman's reflections, and at any time during the meeting someone asks for it.
8. In between meetings, we connect with each other in order to help one another continue to explore the questions of the N.E.W. process, and offer support as needed. We especially reach out to those who are new to the circle meetings and process.
9. We want to reach out to as many women as possible in order to accomplish the vision of N.E.W. Therefore, we meet in a public location, safe, free of interruption, and open to any woman who wishes to attend.

We may collect a small fee at the meeting to defray any expenses.

The time frame can be as short as an hour once a week, or a couple

Of hours once or twice a month.

We cover one of the Questions at each meeting, and repeat the cycle of Nine Questions as often as desired.

Ideally, there are NEW circles meeting in many places at many times so that a woman can always find one when she wants it.

THE NINE QUESTION PROCESS (PARTICIPANTS MAY CHOOSE ONE OR MORE PARTS OF A QUESTION THAT HAS MORE THAN ONE PART.)

1. What am I grateful to have survived? Accomplished? Who or what has empowered me in my life so far?

2. What damaging, false beliefs about myself and/or women do I want to release?
   What healing, helpful beliefs do I want to affirm and live?
3. How have I found and followed my own Inner Authority?
   How will I continue to do so?
4. What are the spiritual practices and resources that empower me?
5. What obstacles to using my innate power as a woman have I/we encountered? What are some strategies for dealing with them? How do I stop giving away my power?
6. What can I imagine, and what do I want for my flourishing and the flourishing of all?
7. What concrete actions could I/we take to manifest what I/we want?
8. How can I live with greater connection and support with women and girls in my circles, community, and the world?
9. Free choice

EXPLORING QUESTION NINE:

Free Choice!

From a bowl of boiled eggs in the Center, each woman, in turns takes one egg, and while holding it, shares what question she has chosen to explore as part of the N.E.W. process.

After she is done, she takes a marker or pen or pencil from the Center, and draws a question mark, her initials, and if she wishes, a symbol of her question on the egg.

Then she puts her egg in the bowl. The next woman does the same thing, and so on, until everyone has had a chance to speak, and to draw their initials, a question mark, and perhaps a symbol on one of the eggs. Finally, the bowl of eggs is passed, and each woman puts her initials on every egg, so that at the end, every woman has an egg initialed by everyone in the circle as a symbol of their support, and empowerment.

This meeting ends with a celebration, perhaps planned by some of the circle members in advance. It can include music, dancing, good food, etc.

And the spiral of the N.E.W. circle begins again, going deeper and wider into each question, and empowering each woman who participates even more . . .

? ? ? ? ? ? ? ? ?

End notes: The time between this meeting and the next one, when the process begins again with Question One is a good time to focus on inviting women who have not yet attended to join a N.E.W. circle, and try out the process for themselves.

Whether it is by word of mouth only, or by announcements in a local newspaper, fliers in local places where women who might be interested stop by, or by email, let the light of your circle shine so women who need and want empowerment can find you. That is how N.E.W. will grow. And if the circle has gotten large, it would be a good idea for a couple members to start another circle, at a different time or location, so that there are more opportunities for women in your community to find a N.E.W. circle convenient for them. You have all you need to keep going and keep growing. So go for it!

Copies of these N.E.W. circle meeting guides can also be found on the website at *www.networktoempowerwomen.com* so that you can print them up and run them off for use in the circles you are a part of or begin.

THE FUTURE FOR WOMEN - A N.E.W. BOOK